The Problem with Being Perfect

From The United Federation Of Asian Perfect-ness

Friends In High Places

"Wayne Chan is delightfully funny and amazingly on target. It's the stuff you may think but would never say out loud. His reflections on everyday life as an Asian American are thoughtful, insightful, warm, and never ever boring! Enjoy!!"

Cheryl Weiberg, Editor-in-Chief, Asian Pages

"For seven years, Wayne Chan has enriched the lives of the 200,000 readers of ASIA, The Journal of Culture & Commerce, with columns that capture the foibles, the heartaches, the joy and the thrill of being a husband, father, and observer of the quirkier things in life. Whether he is writing about the smelliest fruit in Asia, or the meaning of his grandfather's life, Wayne's writings have enriched us all. They capture what we all have experienced, but have never really observed quite the way he does. How many times, after reading one of his columns, have we said to ourselves: "Yeah, I never looked at it that way." With the keen eye of a writer, Wayne shares those special nuances. But more importantly he brings to all of us something we can use every day in troubled as well as good times -- a smile."

Leonard Novarro, Co-publisher, ASIA, The Journal of Culture & Commerce.

The Problem With Being Perfect

From The United Federation Of Asian Perfect-ness

Written by

Wayne Chan

Illustrations by the *other*

Wayne Chan

AuthorHouse™
1663 Liberty Drive
Bloomington, IN 47403
www.authorhouse.com
Phone: 1-800-839-8640

© 2010 Wayne Chan. All rights reserved.

No part of this book may be reproduced, stored in a retrieval system, or transmitted by any means without the written permission of the author.

First published by AuthorHouse 3/26/2010

ISBN: 978-1-4490-9354-9 (sc)
ISBN: 978-1-4490-9355-6 (hc)
ISBN: 978-1-4490-9356-3 (e)

Library of Congress Control Number: 2010904357

Printed in the United States of America
Bloomington, Indiana

This book is printed on acid-free paper.

To my parents, Shu-Yun & Lillian,

who gave me everything I needed

&

My wife Maya,

who makes everything possible

Contents

Introduction	viii
Chinese Family Reunion Dinners 101	1
Two Waynes are Better than One	5
A Tale of Forbidden Fruit	8
Birthdays a Case of Diminishing Returns	11
The Bathrooms are Alive with the Sound of Music	13
A Promise to Keep - A Letter To My Daughter	16
Whatever Doesn't Kill You Makes You Stronger	18
Then There's the One About the Herd of Meatballs	21
For One Family, a Different Kind of Shell Game	24
One Man's Medicine is the Same Man's Embarassment	27
A Sweltering Problem Begs for a Cool Solution	30
Like Comparing Apples to Puttymoo	33
The Seven Habits of Highly Effective Asians	36
Getting a Jump on the Competition, Unless You're Playing Checkers with Your Son	40
Bless You, Yao Ming, Bless You	43
An Unexpected Gift	46
A Belt-Free Vacation	49
Time Marches On, Unless You Uninvite Yourself	52
Working Out a Pointless Exercise	54
The Benefits Of Being The Human Pretzel	57
The United Federation of Asian Perfect-ness	59
Anniversary of Diminishing Returns	61
Apologies For a Twenty Five Year Old Wedgie	65
A Meat and No Potatoes Kind of Guy	67
A Massage to Die For	69
The Britney and Beijing Accord	72
Would You Like That With a Side of Grits or an Egg Roll?	74
Inner Peace - Yes, Outer Silence…No Way	76
Coming Soon - Casa de Vietnam	78
Mother Nature Calls - for Gloves And Goggles	81
How Not To Become My Own Zipcode	85
Bruce Lee or James Bond –That is the Question	88
A General's Generational Tale	90
Watch Your Language; It May Save You (Asia Trip - Part One)	93
Unaccustomed to Customs Checkpoints (Asia Trip - Part Two)	95
Learning the ABC's of Chinese - Minus the ABC's	97
The Kitchen God and His Missing Dumplings	99
Crouching Child, Bedeviled Parent	101
Dressed to the Nines - or Maybe Just Four and a Half	104
A Duck for the Ages	106
Eight Words of Wisdom	108
Eliminating the Gray Area	111
A Time for Reflection, Resolutions, and Calcium Supplements	114
English is Perfect – Know What I mean?	116

Not a Cloud in the Sky - on Purpose 118
A Bouncing Ball and a Bruised Ego 120
Not the Best or Worst of Times – But Somewhere in the Middle 122
A Picture Perfect Picture a Pain to Perfect 124
A Picture is Worth a Thousand Edits 127
A Tour Guide of the Mundane 130
Born Without a Funny Bone 132
Dazed and Confused in a Shopping Mall 135
A Complex Simplicity 137
The American Dream - Transplanted 139
The Michael Jordan of Sons 145
The Dog Days of 2006 148
Hogging Up All The Attention for Chinese New Year 150
The Year of the Adorable Rodent 152
From Noodles to Burgers & Back 154
The Anti-Asian Stereotype Man 157
Turning Nothing Into a Political Career 159
To Golf Or Not To Golf - That Is The Problem 161
Justice In The Name Of Purple 164
General Tso - Your Check is in the Mail 166
Maybe We Could Create a Dessert Called TIR-AH-MAH-SU 168
A Home of Good Fortune and Little Patience 170
To Beard or not to Beard 172
Fish, Fish, Where For Art Thou Fish? 174
No Crab, But a Barrel Full of Excuses 176
Dental Work Via Hand Signals 179
Yogurt Schmogurt – I'll Take Chocolate 181
Blaming Parents for a Happy Childhood 183
The Wild Kingdom - In My Yard 185
A Dedication to San Diego's Fire Fighters 188
Giving a Whole New Meaning to Monkey Business 190
Kope Coffee Truly Scat-terbrained Idea 193

Introduction

Writing, by it's very nature, is a process bound in isolation. Any writer, whether they are writing the next great American novel, or in my case, trying to describe in vivid detail the experience of being walked on by a heavy set masseuse, creates their work alone.

A writer writes alone, usually in a quiet room, away from any potential distractions. Yet, it's what happens outside that room that ends up being the subject of most of my writing.

For example, a few days ago, I fell down a long spiral staircase. It took me so long to fall down these stairs that I actually had time to think about things on the way down.

How long is this going to take? Why do I keep wearing socks when I know how slippery these stairs are? I wonder if my kids are watching me falling down these stairs? How can I only be halfway down these stairs? After I'm done falling, should I immediately scream or should I quickly take my socks off so my wife can't tell me how many times she's told me that I shouldn't wear socks when I'm on the stairs? How much longer is this going to take?

These are the types of topics that I write about in my syndicated column. And yet, since I'm rarely present when someone is reading my column to get their feedback, I sometimes make an effort to make sure that people are still interested in what I'm thinking when I'm falling down a set of stairs.

A few years ago I started attending some writer's conferences to see what other people were writing. This conference happened to be the Erma Bombeck Writer's Workshop held every other year in Dayton, Ohio. One of the workshops was called something like, "How a Writer Finds Their Voice".

My understanding is that a writer's voice is the perspective of a writer as well as their individual writing style. Finding your "voice" is essential for any writer.

Even after I started writing my column, I have wondered whether the perspective of an Asian American writer, particularly one that was writing about, let's face it - drivel, was a good "voice" for a writer.

As I sat down for the "Voices" workshop, I noticed that of the 200 or so writers in the room, I was the only Asian in the room. Not only that, I was the only non-white person in the room.

Towards the end of the presentation describing several helpful exercises to help writers find their "voice", there was a question and answer period. After a few others took their turn, I raised my hand.

Hi. My name is Wayne Chan. I write a syndicated humor column, and I write from an Asian American perspective and tend to write fluff pieces about eating "Sushi on a stick" at the county fair or how I once used hand signals to communicate to my dentist of what to do to me since he didn't understand English or Chinese. Do you think my "voice" is one that people will want to hear?

After a brief pause, the presenter said, "Look around you Wayne. Everyone here is *looking* for their voice. You have one sitting in your lap. Go for it."

I've been following his advice ever since.

This book is a collection of my work, primarily my columns, and a few personal items I wanted to share. Many of the columns are accompanied by a comic drawn by my friend and collaborator, Wayne Chan. And no, I am not so high minded that I'm referring to myself in third person. Read on and you'll understand.

I hope you enjoy our fun. Thank you so much for taking the time to read it.

Excuse me, but I need to go downstairs to get something. Wish me luck.

Chinese Family Reunion Dinners 101

For those of you who may attend a Chinese banquet or are Chinese and are planning a big get together with family, I have compiled a set of guidelines that should help you in your preparation.

My qualifications? My parents have 17 brothers and sisters among them. Growing up, I attended so many family reunions that I sometimes wondered when the separation occurred that justified having another family reunion.

With that said, here are some helpful hints on how to proceed, in chronological order:

1. You must select a restaurant (Chinese, of course), in the most concentrated part of town, on a busy Friday night (in your local Chinatown), preferably with no free parking in the vicinity that will force you to drive past a number of pay parking lots in order to park free in a dimly lit alleyway close to a neighborhood pawn shop.

2. Once you have arrived, you must make sure the restaurant you have chosen has ambient noise loud enough to drown out any kind of meaningful conversation. After all, this is a family reunion. It's not the time or place for any kind of small talk.

3. Once the restaurant has been chosen, adults are seated at one table and children sit at another. All tables are round and large enough to seat approximately 15 people. All children must sit at one table, regardless of how many are in attendance. If there are so many children that some must share a seat or play "tag-team dining", so be it.

4. The first big test of the evening is in ordering the appropriate dishes. The dishes ordered for the adults must be so expensive that you may need to get a second mortgage on your home to pay for it. However, it is important for you to give the impression that you always eat this way, as if you normally order shark fin soup at $150/bowl. This image projects success.

   It is also a good idea to order something off the menu in which the animal of choice is cooked whole and presented in it's entirety for the enjoyment of the guests. As a rule of thumb, the larger the carcass, the better.

   Dishes for the adult table are seafood based. On the other hand, dishes for the kid's table are carbohydrate based. The dishes for the children must include vast quantities of starch, particularly rice and noodles. Non-carbohydrate based dishes, such as sweet and sour pork, should include the smallest bits of the toughest meat possible, covered with a thick layering of starch, and then deep-fried beyond recognition. As a side note, the meat within the starch must be so small as to make it difficult to detect or taste until you have flossed later in the evening and dislodged it from between your teeth.

   Although it is hard to find, a children's specialty would be a dish of nuggets made entirely of starch, then covered with flour batter, deep fried and covered with a gooey, sugary red sauce which should eliminate any nutritional value whatsoever.

Finally, for budgeting purposes, the dollar ratio between dishes served for the adults vs. children should be approximately 35 to one.

5. When the first dishes arrive, it is best to ask the waitress to slow everything down so as to make each course a test in patience. Chinese tradition dictates that true prosperity allows the family the luxury to slowly enjoy their meal. If, in the course of your meal, you notice that the newspaper delivery boy is going about his rounds, you have accomplished your task.

6. During the meal, the role of all those who attend is to show mock amazement and to beseech the host that they have ordered too much. This is a customary ritual designed to convey the guest's observation that the host has enough money to feed a small army. The host must respond in kind by ordering five more dishes.

    Another Chinese custom is to communicate your pleasure in the dishes by eating as loudly as possible. This conveys the pleasure you are experiencing to your gracious host. Once the sound level of smacking lips and gums begins to sound like a chorus of tap dancers, you have made your feelings known.

7. Towards the end of the meal, the roles of the elders in the party are somewhat different. It is their responsibility to grade each dish based on how much they disliked it. The grading scale is between a B- and a D, and it is customary to add some judicial comment along with their evaluation. Comments such as "The fish in that dish is too fishy tasting" or "This **used** to be one of their specialties" are always acceptable observations.

8. After the last dish is finished, toothpicks are handed out so that everyone in the party can join in a round of teeth cleaning. Of course, etiquette demands that while one hand is poking and prodding, the other hand covers the mouth to obstruct any direct viewing by others seated at the table.

9. At the end of the meal, the waitress will promptly present a bill for the evening's festivities. It is at this point that at least two or three of those in attendance must argue over who will pay for the dinner. The

negotiations that ensue must be loud, insistent, and unwavering. It is customary and even suggested that someone grab the bill and walk towards the waitress with the intent to pay. It is also appropriate for the other person to follow him and grab their shoulder in order to continue bickering. However, tripping the person as they are walking up with the bill is considered to be stepping over the lines of proper etiquette.

One simple tip to help determine how fervently you should fight over the bill: For the most part, the less money you make, the more insistent you should be to pick up the tab. This is called, "Being in denial".

10. On the drive back home with each family going their separate ways, it is appropriate for the adults in the car to repeatedly question, "Why do we always have to go through the same thing every time we get together?" The children, slouched in the back seat and stuffed to their ears in carbs, should promptly respond by burping in unison.

Two Waynes are Better than One

The Waynes of the World

I'd like to apologize to my parents.

I have done my best to be a good son. I went to college, and even went on to get a masters degree, despite the fact that I went through it reluctantly. At the time, I think I made a very good case for not going to college.

Let's see – my reasons were:

1. I'm not going to learn anything useful in college that I don't already know now. Why do I need to learn calculus?
2. I'm going to be the world's number one tennis player. What do I need college for?
3. I'm already making plenty of money being the "Dough Specialist" at Round Table Pizza.

After listening to my thoughtful reasoning and very sound logic, I believe my mom's response was, "I don't want to hear it. You're going."

Now that some time has passed, I can see my parents were right (although I still have never been in a situation where calculus came in handy). In every respect, I owe my parents for everything I have in my life.

But right now, I owe them an apology. Let me explain.

I don't like my name. "Wayne Chan" – two one word syllables. It's too short. It sounds like a doorbell chime.

Obviously, there's not that much that my parents could do with my last name. But "Wayne"? Is that the best they could come up with? Why not something more macho like "Bronson"? With a name like that, I'd go around introducing myself to strangers just so I could say my own name.

Yes, the name's Chan – Bronson Chan. Please, just call me Bronson.

You don't like "Bronson"? That's fine, there are a lot of other names that I would be perfectly happy with. How about "Daniel"? I'd be fine being Daniel Chan, despite the fact that you can't shake a stick without hitting another Chinese guy named "Daniel". Why not? It's a nice name.

But "Wayne"? Where did that name come from? Actually, I know the answer to that question. I once looked up the etymology for my first name. According to my research, the name "Wayne" was an old English occupational surname that meant, "Wagon maker."

I doubt that my parents were actually thinking about 18th century modes of transportation when they were trying to name their son, but maybe I'm just not giving them their due credit.

All of this leads to the real reason I've written this column. Several weeks ago I came upon a young man who pens a number of comic strips, many of them drawn from the perspective of an Asian American. I think his work is truly terrific.

We got to talk and we thought it would be a perfect match if we worked together, combining my columns and his strips. We work in different mediums – I write columns, and he draws comic strips, but we do share a commonality in our perspectives – as Asian Americans who find humor in our daily lives.

So, without further ado, let me introduce (and I am not making this up)... Wayne Chan.

Wayne is based in the Bay Area, and yes, the strip you see next to this column is by him. We'd like to name our collaboration – column & comic strip, "The Waynes of the World." We hope you enjoy it.

By the way, Wayne, if you're reading this – I guess I owe your parents an apology too.

A Tale of Forbidden Fruit

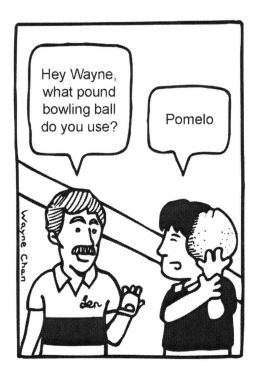

As a service to our readers, I have taken it upon myself, in a never-ending quest to unravel the secrets of Asian culture, to seek out and uncover, at some personal risk to myself, the mysteries of Asia's forbidden fruits.

That's right – I'm here to tell you about all the weird fruit they have on sale at my local Asian supermarket.

Now, it's fortunate that I've been able to travel to Asia frequently and I've seen the variety of fruit available over there. There's nothing in the Asian markets here that I haven't seen for sale over there. Still, I can imagine the initial shock of anyone walking through the produce section of an Asian supermarket for the first time.

Let's take the pomelo, for example. A pomelo is the largest fruit in the citrus family. The term "large" is an understatement.

How big is it?

A typical pomelo is roughly the same size as a full-grown golden retriever. I once saw a pomelo fall off a fruit stand and roll down a grocery aisle forcing women and children to flee in horror from the marauding citrus boulder rolling towards them. A family of four could live off of one pomelo for a week and a half. In some countries when you file your taxes you can claim your pomelo as a dependent.

It's that BIG.

Rambutan is a fruit from Southeast Asia that has a very pleasant taste and is shaped similarly to lychee, except that the outside shell is round and covered with soft, crimson red tentacles. I don't know how else to describe the look of rambutan except to say that it seems oddly perverted. When holding rambutan in your hand at a local Asian supermarket, I have a tendency to look over my shoulder to see if anyone's looking in my direction as if I'm doing something seedy.

The few times I've purchased rambutan at the market I've discreetly asked the bagger to stuff them into a plain, brown paper bag.

Then there's the durian. A durian is about the size and shape of a football covered with sharp, spiny, green thorns on the outside, looking a lot like a grenade on steroids. Cutting a durian in half, you see two sacs, each filled with a grayish yellow gelatinous mass that looks a lot like the forensics scene from the movie Aliens.

Let's not forget about the famous durian smell. Encyclopedia Britannica describes the durian smell as a "pungent foul odor." How would I describe it? Take one pair of dirty gym socks, stuff them with some moldy cheese, drive them to your nearest dairy farm during the warmest time of the day, and *voilà! Pungent foul odor.*

Despite the fact that the actual taste of a durian is sweet and creamy, what puzzles me is that some point at the beginning of time, one of our ancestors came upon this ominous looking fruit for the first time with all it's spiny thorns, alien-like innards, and locker room smell, and was still curious enough (or desperate enough) to wonder, "Sure - it's scary looking and smells like my feet, but I wonder what it tastes like?"

Maybe he was so famished and exhausted from lugging around the pomelo he found that he was ready to eat anything.

Birthdays a Case of Diminishing Returns

Ahh…sweet memories.

It seems not so long ago that I celebrated my 30th birthday. I remember it fondly.

A surprise party. All my best friends and family in attendance. A beautiful cake. My lovely wife, presenting me with my favorite cake from my favorite bakery with several candles on top to mark the occasion. The opening of hand picked presents from the people closest to me and the singing of of "Happy Birthday" in a joyous celebration of this personal milestone.

Good times.

Fast forward 14 years. A few of the details have changed. Oh, I still have a beautiful wife, and there was a cake. But, as they say, the devil is in the details.

My birthday dinner plans were cobbled together in a couple of minutes the day before my birthday. On the day of the joyous event, my wife calls and tells me she doesn't have time to buy any candles and asks me to pick some up on my way to my parent's house.

Yes, you read that right. I must run out to buy candles for my own birthday cake.

Dinner goes well, and as always, our family always enjoys opportunities to get together. For dessert, the birthday cake is brought out, and this year the cake is not the one from my favorite bakery, but is instead a store bought cake from our local supermarket. I know this because the price sticker is still on the cellophane of the cake box and in addition, I remember seeing the same cake earlier in the day as I was shopping for candles.

As the candles flicker on top of my ready-made cake, I prepare to blow them out. But before I do, my mother stops me and says that we must not forget that my sister in law's birthday is just a few days later and that we are celebrating for her as well.

There is a slight pause as I wait to see if she would like to "bundle" any other milestones or holidays under the auspices of what is quickly becoming known as the "all encompassing celebratory cake" as I note that "Groundhog Day" is only a few weeks away.

While it may not be hard for any of you to pick up on the latent bitterness as I recall my last birthday celebration, the truth is that I found the change to be more funny than anything else. I don't really have anything to complain about as I have a terrific wife and family.

Still, it's not hard to extrapolate what lies ahead of me as I look ahead to my future birthday celebrations.
On my 50th birthday, all my friends and family will come to celebrate this major milestone in my life, topped off by a beautiful, home made cake festooned with candles and other festive decorations. Of course, by that time I figure that I'll be the one baking the cake so why not give it my all?

On my 60th birthday, we will most likely drop the whole "celebratory cake" thing and the formal celebration will entail me trying some of the free samples at Costco as I shop for my sister in law's birthday cake.

They do sell candles there, right?

The Bathrooms are Alive with the Sound of Music

THOSE **USED TO** BE MY FAVORITE SONGS.

I have decided to be a brain surgeon.

I have no relevant experience or formal training as a brain surgeon, but I do have some time on my hands and thought it might be challenging and fun. I'll probably kick off my new role as a brain surgeon this weekend with something manageable – nothing too demanding.

Wait a minute. Did I say I wanted to be a "Brain Surgeon"? I'm sorry... that's just silly. What I meant to say was "Karaoke Singer". There's not really that much in common between the two. First off, Karaoke singers don't usually hold people's lives in the palm of their hands. Hearing? Possibly. But lives? Probably not.

For those who don't know, Karaoke (pronounced "Carry-Okey" in the West) is the popular phenomenon that began in Japan where patrons take turns singing lyrics to pre-recorded music.

I have participated in Karaoke both here and in Asia. While the experience in the U.S. is fairly straightforward, out in Asia it is much more elaborate. For those of you who might have an opportunity to Karaoke in Asia, I thought I might provide the following observations as a primer.

Karaoke Clubs are often located in posh hotels throughout Asia. Once you enter the lobby of a club, you are greeted by a hostess dressed in formal attire who will escort you to a private and elegantly decorated Karaoke room. You are somewhat surprised by all the pomp and circumstance surrounding an activity that is typically reserved for your daily shower.

You and your friends enter a small room lined with an "L" shaped sofa on one end facing a large screen on the other. The more exclusive rooms also include an adjoining restroom in case nature calls or can be used as a makeshift "quiet room" for those who would rather miss the least talented member of the group straining to hit the high notes of "New York, New York" (" *These little town blues are melting awaaaaay!*").

Once seated on the sofa, a waiter will take drink and snack orders. While the Karaoke room charges are very reasonable, you suspect that the club makes up the difference on what they charge for food and drinks. Either that, or there must be a world wide potato and barley shortage forcing the club to charge eighteen dollars for a bag of potato chips and a beer.

The next order of business is to select songs for everyone to sing. Seeing as how this is a Chinese Karaoke club, most of the songs are in Chinese, but a good number of them are from the west as well.

As far as I can tell, all Chinese Karaoke songs are about love. There are songs about being in love, falling in love, falling out of love, looking for love, finding love, songs by singer Courtney Love, tennis matches with a score of 15-love, words that start with "L" that rhyme with "dove"…you definitely start to see a pattern.

As for me, I never have to worry about selecting a song. Like it or not, in the course of the evening I will inevitably end up singing the Righteous Brother's "Unchained Melody." For some reason, if you are from America and have been invited to a Karaoke party in Asia, you are required to sing that song. I believe you have to agree to it before they'll issue you a visa.

On top of that, the person operating the Karaoke machine always raises the pitch of the song, so the only way I can reach the high notes is if I'm wearing some really tight pants. By the time I reach the climax of the song and reach that last high note, no one can hear me except for any stray dogs or dolphins that happen to be near by.

Although the written word can hardly do it justice, I thought I'd give you a sampling of my performance of that final verse:

" I-aye-aye-aye NEED your love!!!"
"I-aye-aye-aye-aye need your luh-huv,"
"God speed your love, to-who-who-who-ooh, me-HEE-HEE-EEE!!!"

The bathroom really gets hoppin' when I get to that part.

A Promise to Keep
– A Letter To My Daughter

To my beautiful girl,

It has taken me quite a while to bring myself to write you this letter. I write this to you now in the hopes that many years from now, with a lot of hard work, patience, and no small measure of luck, this will be a faint reminder of the past.

It has been several months now since we first learned of your diagnosis. Learning that your child has the telltale symptoms of autism has affected both your mother and I in different ways.

It has hit your mother the hardest. I married your mother because of the way she lives her life. She has a beautiful heart – simple, innocent and pure. She's worried about your future. She's worried about your future if and when we aren't here to care for you. She is sacrificing everything she has to provide for you.

While I support everything your mother is doing for you, because it will help – I see you walking down a different path.

From everything I have read about this condition, it is like each child has a door to open. It's a door to your consciousness, a door to your being. It's a door to you.

For whatever reason, God has made your door a little heavier – a little harder to unlock. Yet with each passing day, your mother and I are pushing a little harder on the door, and some times you manage to peek your head part way through. While it sometimes only lasts for a second, we see you struggling as hard to come out as we are trying to get in. Yet for each of those moments, we can see that the potential and promise is worth every effort.

A few days ago you told us you wanted to watch Elmo. Just the other day when mom asked you where her nose was, you showed her and pointed at her nose as if you had known for years. You laughed and mom cried, yet you were both happy.

You are already a beautiful child. I have no doubt in my mind that you will be a beautiful grownup. I believe when all is said and done, you will surprise everyone – including me.

Regardless of what the future brings, as your Dad, I have signed on for the duration. You should know that you will never go hungry, be without shelter, or be without love. As long as I draw a breath and even beyond that, you will be cared for.

Let me be more specific.

When you start walking to school on your own, try not to mind the gray-haired fellow hiding behind every bush or sign behind you. He just wants you to show him the way.

When you start to read and run into one of those hard words, come to me. I probably won't know it either but at least I'll help you find the dictionary.

When you start to play soccer, softball, or make the cheerleading squad, try not to mind the gray-haired fellow jumping up and down in the stands. He is your cheerleader.

If there is any time you can't do something even when all your friends can, let me know. You can do it.

These are some of the promises your mother and I have made. I am sure we'll make up some more along the way.

The door will open soon enough. Good morning, sweetheart. Wake up, come out and play. It's beautiful out here.

Whatever Doesn't Kill You Makes You Stronger

Warrior Chan from the "Whatever-doesn't-kill-you-makes-you-stronger" dynasty.

I've always wondered where that expression started. Nowadays, the expression is reserved for people who have overcome an obstacle or endured a hardship.

But, it's not usually used in a truly life threatening situation. I doubt the first thing you'll hear when you see a guy get run over by a bus is, "Somebody call a doctor! I hope he's OK. Well, you know what they say…"

I have my own theories on where that expression started. My guess is that the expression was coined the first time someone was experimenting with some new discovery.

It could have been an engineer testing automobile air bags for the first time before someone else had discovered "crash test dummies". Maybe it was the first person to try cooking metal in a microwave.

My own guess is that it started with some medical advancement hundreds, maybe even thousands of years ago. I wonder if some ancient medicine man in Asia might have uttered this now famous expression the same day they discovered acupuncture.

Now, before anyone starts writing me e-mails on why I'm poking fun (pun intended) at an ancient and proven method of eastern medicine, let me just say that I absolutely believe in the benefits of acupuncture as well as all other alternative Asian remedies. My only question is what motivated the first person to come up with the idea of sticking sharp objects into ones body for medicinal purposes?

I've got a raging headache. I wonder what would happen if I shoved this huge needle into my toe?

What I am poking fun at (OK, now I'm just being redundant) is how this alternative medicine came to be. At some point, thousands of years ago, I imagine a poor guy with some painful malady went in to see the village healer.

At some point in the diagnosis, the village healer must have said something like this to the patient:

Village Healer: OK. I see the problem. You have a hernia. We will have to operate. Let me give you your choices. In the past, our only choice to curb the pain during surgery was to take a huge mallet and knock you senseless with it until you are out. While you are still, we perform the procedure. You'll heal from the surgery in a couple of days but it might take you a few weeks to wake up and recover from the beating.

Patient: Village healer, you said I had a choice. What is the *alternative* to the mallet? (hence the term, *alternative* medicine).

Village Healer: The alternative is a new procedure we've been looking at where we insert these sharp needles into your body in an attempt to block out the pain signals from reaching your brain. However, since this is the first time we've attempted this and don't know what goes where, we're going to have to poke around until we hit the right nerve. Since this is experimental, I would still recommend going with the mallet.

The patient spends the next few minutes shifting glances between the mallet and a huge pincushion while the village healer impatiently looks at his sundial while waiting for a decision.

Village Healer: Well, have you made up your mind?

Patient: Umm...I think I'll just keep the hernia.

Village Healer: Nonsense. Look, whatever doesn't kill you, makes you stronger.

And with that, an expression was born.

Then There's the One About the Herd of Meatballs

Don't believe everything you read. If there's anything you might take away after reading this column, I hope you believe that simple fact.

Hmm...I think there's something wrong with my point, but I just can't put my finger on it.

Anyways, the point I was trying to make is about how in this day and age, the internet allows anyone who has a keyboard to write just about anything they'd like for public consumption, which makes it tougher for everyone to discern fact from fiction.

Case in point: The mystery of the genetic robo super-chicken.

My father is a very educated and wise man. He came to this country from China nearly penniless, and yet he's gone on to become a respected university professor, written a text book, and owned several businesses. He and my mother managed to raise my brother and I, support us through college and send us on our way to make our own lives.

Yet for most of his life, as with most people of his generation, when they read something in a newspaper, book, or magazine, they could usually trust that the information they were reading had been thoroughly vetted by an editor or publisher.

So you can understand how an errant e-mail might distort my dad's "reality field".

Let me just say, before I begin, that I did not make the following up.

Not so long ago, a friend of the family forwarded an e-mail to my dad with a disturbing report. The e-mail, written entirely in Chinese, claimed that Kentucky Fried Chicken (now known as KFC), in an effort to cut costs and boost profit margins, had managed to genetically alter the DNA of a chicken so that these new chickens no longer had feathers, bones, a beak, wings, legs, or heads.

Essentially, KFC had created a living, breathing, full-sized chicken nugget.

Upon further investigation, I was astonished to learn that when these boneless blobs of chicken roll around vigorously in their chicken coops, they sweat honey mustard sauce.

OK, OK, I just made up that last part. But, it's not like after reading about this robo-chicken that someone's going to read my little fib and say, "OK Wayne, **now** you're just being silly!"

Seeing as how my father has always loved eating at Kentucky Fried Chicken (as does all of the Chan family, which probably has something to do with **his** DNA being passed along to all of **us**), he was immediately taken aback and aghast.

In fact, he was so repulsed by what he had read that it prompted him to write a letter to the president of KFC to seek out the truth.

In his letter to the president of KFC, my Dad wrote:

Dear Sir,

I have enjoyed eating KFC products for many years. However, I am writing to you today because of an e-mail I recently received that deeply troubles me. The claim I've read is that the reason Kentucky Fried Chicken has changed it's name to KFC is because KFC no longer serves real chickens.

I would appreciate it if you would respond to these allegations so that I might be able to continue enjoying your products.

Thank you.

Surprisingly enough, KFC did manage to reply to my dad's thoughtful letter. In it, they assert that this rumor was an urban legend and that KFC serves the same type of chickens that we all might buy at our local markets.

Fair enough. The only problem I have with their explanation is that it doesn't exactly give me a vote of confidence when the last time I visited the supermarket I bought a big tube of boneless ground chicken.

For One Family, A Different Kind of Shell Game

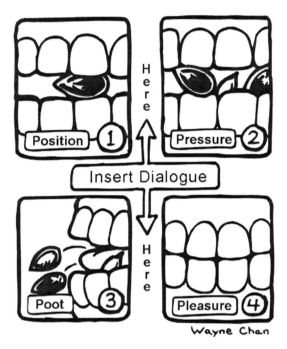

The Tao of Shell-Shucking

Yesterday as I was lounging about in front of the TV, I came across a scene that reminded me how resourceful, skilled, and talented we humans can be.

To be specific, it wasn't anything I saw on television that amazed me. No, what amazed me was watching my relatives in the dining room across from me eating sunflower seeds.

You can learn a lot about social interaction simply by watching the way people eat - especially when they're eating seeds.

Part of my fascination comes from the efficient way Asians eat seeds. Unlike westerners, who tend to hold the seed in their hand, bite the seed to split the shell and eat the seed inside, Asians are more efficient. Asians have a patented technique whereby several seeds are placed in the mouth and via a rigorous motion between tongue and teeth, each individual sunflower seed is shucked, shell separated, spit out, and seed digested.

While this technique has been handed down from generation to generation, you can still tell that some concentration is required, simply by looking at the facial expression of the person eating the seed.

By closely observing the seed-eating individual, you will immediately find that the various parts of the face appear to be focused on different tasks. Obviously, the mouth carries the lions share of the work, which you can tell by noting that the person's lips are continuously pursed, moving from side to side in a vigorous motion, except for a moment every ten seconds or so when the mouth erupts in a violent motion, ejecting the shell of the seed as if it were some foreign object invading the body.

[Author's Note: As a point of caution, it is strongly recommended that any person seeking to observe this hull-spitting maneuver do so from a safe distance – say ten feet – and wearing protective goggles wouldn't be a bad idea either.]

While the mouth is preoccupied with what I call the "Shell-Shuck" maneuver, the eyes have an altogether different role. During the "Shell-Shucking" process, the job of the eyes is to dart back and forth, eyebrows furrowed in a serious gaze, with an expression that suggests that there could be a surprise any moment, with each individual seed.

Perhaps the eyes are anticipating that the next shell could come up empty without a seed. The technical term for this result is being "shell-shocked."

Beyond sunflower seeds, the variety of seeds Asians eat is impressive. Along with sunflower seeds, a typical seed-eating diet can consist of watermelon seeds, pumpkin seeds, and several other seeds I've never seen before.

The smallest seeds, such as the watermelon seed, create the most questions for me. In my opinion, when eating watermelon seeds, once the shell is removed, the microscopic seed is more likely to become lodged between your teeth before the tongue ever gets a chance to taste it. By my calculations, a fully-grown adult, at one sitting, could polish off the seeds of every watermelon on earth, then eat a ham and cheese sandwich, before this person might ever utter the words, "I'm full."

Besides my fascination with my family's sunflower eating prowess, the other part that amazes me are all the other things people can do while eating seeds. Speaking, in particular, while eating seeds, shows the true multi-tasking nature of seed-eaters.

As complex as eating a sunflower seed is without your hands, people still believe that they can manage to have an intelligent conversation at the same time.

Auntie #1: So, what did…Sue…<*smack, smack*> say after she got <*smack*> home?
Auntie #2: Well, she…<*smuck*> wasn't very happy <*POOT!!!!!*>
Auntie #1 (moving to the other side of the table and refastening her protective goggles): I just think she needs to control her <*POOT! POOT!!!*> temper!

I wonder whether this multi-tasking can be used in other ways? I wonder, along with eating all sorts of seeds, whether this time honored skill could be used on other products, like say, shucking oysters? I bet my aunt could open an oyster, shuck the shell, eat the meat, and maybe even polish the pearl before shooting it out with a celebratory "POOT!"

Yes, yes, I know. You could call this maneuver the ability to "shell fish."

One Man's Medicine is the Same Man's Embarassment

I just came back from a business trip in Beijing and all I got was a lousy T-shirt.

Actually, I didn't bring back any T-shirts. Instead, what I came back with was a sense of amazement.

Sky-high skyscrapers. Locals dressed in the latest couture. Mercedes Benz cars parked next to trendy microbreweries.

Even factory workers would drink Starbucks during their coffee breaks.

OK, a little creative license there, but you see where I'm going with this.

This wasn't the Beijing that I remembered. The last time I visited Beijing, it was 1980. Beijing was so much different. But then again, so was I.

In the summer of 1980, I was 16 years old and I joined a group of students from all over the country to attend a Chinese language program at Beijing's prestigious Tsinghua University.

My parents thought this trip would be a good opportunity for me to learn about my roots. They thought this trip would give me a chance to expand my Chinese language skills. They thought I would come back with a greater appreciation of my heritage and the richness of my culture.

I thought it would be a good chance to meet girls. After all, I and every other student who attended the program were fully aware that this program was informally known as "The Love Boat."

Unfortunately, I didn't really hook up with any girls during the trip. But as a consolation, I did manage to pick up a severe case of food poisoning.

I shared a dorm room with two of my cousins. Seeing as how they were both younger than me and with even less experience with the fairer sex, this was not the best environment I could have hoped for. The room had a concrete floor, and each bed was covered completely with mosquito netting. I quickly discovered that the mosquitoes were in abundance, and unless you wanted to unwillingly donate a pint of blood each night via a hundred mosquito bites, you stayed under the netting.

However, this being the summer, it was also hot and muggy, with nary an air conditioner in sight. Coupled with the fact that the mosquito netting effectively blocked out any breeze from the windows, you soon came to realize that you had inadvertently duplicated the conditions of a Thanksgiving turkey basting in the oven.

Under these sweltering conditions, a cool, tall glass of water would have really hit the spot. Unfortunately, the best we could do was a bracing cup of hot tea, or boiled hot water kept in a large thermos, which contained so much excess grit and minerals that you felt like you were drinking a cup of watery sand.

Towards the end of my journey in China, I came down with a severe case of food poisoning. High temperature, extreme queasiness, a genuine feeling of hopelessness. No, that's not what the food poisoning did to me, that's how I felt as a number of friends helped me make my way to the University's medical clinic and looked inside.

I felt like I was on the set of M*A*S*H.

Still, how bad could it be? I immediately felt more at ease when the doctor told me I just needed some penicillin. However, I soon realized that what might be good for my health might not be so good for my image.

In front of all my friends, including a few girls I was trying to impress, I nonchalantly asked the doctor where I could pick up the penicillin pills.

The doctor replied, "We don't have penicillin *pills*."

Figuring he meant a penicillin shot, I bravely rolled up my sleeve and said, "OK, no problem. I have had lots of shots before."

The doctor, seeming a little perplexed, looked at me and quietly said, "Umm…we don't give you the shot in your *arm*."

After a few moments, I quickly grasped the situation and asked, "You don't mean to tell me you're going to give me a shot in my…"

When it comes right down to it, buying flowers, writing a romantic poem, seeing a romantic movie…there are a lot of things a young man can do to win a young woman's heart. Bending over and pulling your pants down in front of your friends for a penicillin shot is not one of them.

Then again, the experience certainly wasn't a complete loss. I did manage to learn the Chinese words to ask, "Could somebody please cover me up with a blanket?"

A Sweltering Problem Begs for a Cool Solution

I found out recently that I will be traveling to China sometime in August.

Let the sweating begin.

How hot is it, you ask?

It's a brutally humid, suffocating heat. I suppose it's good that it's humid because if it were a dry heat, visitors like me might spontaneously burst into flames.

It's so hot Chinese tourists spend their summers on African safaris just so they can "beat the heat." It's so hot you can put a bowl of ice outside and watch how the ice just dissipates into the air, bypassing the whole "ice melting" stage.

It's that kind of hot. At least it is for me.

I am quite sure that the last time I traveled to China in the summer, I made a vow that I would never go back to China in the summer. Yet, here I am again, going to China in the summer. I think there's a conspiracy going on between the people issuing Visas and my wife who would like to see me lose some weight.

Of course, China and the rest of Asia have long since discovered air conditioning. It's in all modern buildings, from hotels, restaurants and businesses far and wide. It's just not in any of the places I go when I'm on business.

I've tried everything. I started out bringing a hotel towel with me wherever I went. It didn't really keep me cool but at least I could keep myself from looking like I just came out of a "Singing in the Rain" dance rehearsal.

I once brought a battery-powered fan but that didn't do the trick. I then put my faith in the promise of high technology and bought a battery powered, personal cooling doodad that wraps around your neck and is supposed to keep you cool. Of course, a side effect from wearing this contraption was that it made me look like a complete idiot, but what's a little embarrassment when it comes to my personal comfort?

Unfortunately, it didn't work, so the only thing I accomplished was to give the impression that the latest fad in the west was for grown men to wear shiny new dog collars.

So, in my latest bout of desperation, I have searched far and wide and I believe I've finally come up with the perfect solution to keep me from sweltering in another hot summer in China.

I've asked my brother to go instead of me.

Unfortunately, I'm just kidding. I'm still going, but I do think I may really have solved the problem.
Last week, while surfing on the web, I came across a web site devoted to

products to help soothe sore muscles and other body aches. One of the products was an ice pack that gets ice cold without the use of a freezer or refrigerator. By shaking the bag, the pack goes through some kind of chemical reaction and instantly becomes ice cold for about an hour.

Instant cold? Someone must be smiling down on me.

Of course, reading the fine print on the back of the ice pack has a way of yanking me back to reality. In very tiny print, it reads:

Caution. Ice pack capable of extreme cold. Prolonged exposure can cause redness, swelling, frostbite, possible hypothermia, loss of circulation, and other health issues related to extreme cold.

Of course, let's not forget the added effect of me looking like a complete idiot. But what's a little embarrassment, some swelling, a touch of hypothermia, and a loss of feeling on my neck when it comes to my own personal, umm…where the heck did I put that battery-powered fan?

Like Comparing Apples to Puttymoo

Um...I think we should split.

I have a simple linguistics test for you.

The next time you go out for breakfast, I'd like you to try and order a glass of orange juice as quickly as possible. Simple, right?

Oh, I forgot one important part of the test. Try ordering said glass of juice without anyone using the word, "orange". Aha...not so easy now, huh smarty pants?

Inevitably, the conversation between you and the server will go something like this:

> You: And with my breakfast, I'd like to order a small glass of...uhh...

Server:	Yes?	
You:	I'd like a glass of juice from a certain type of fruit.	
Server:	Of course, no problem. What type of juice would you like?	
You:	Uhh…well, it's a citrus fruit, but not a lemon or a lime. It's round like a grapefruit but not a grapefruit.	
Server:	Hmm…I see. Maybe I can help. What color is the fruit you'd like juice from?	
You:	Color, yes, of course. Well, uh…it's like a darker yellow, or maybe a lighter brown color.	
Server:	I'm sorry, but could you be a bit more specific?	
You:	I don't suppose you have any tangerine juice?	

I bring this up because in the miracle of communication that we call language, a single word like "orange" can make the biggest difference in the world. Unfortunately, I found this out the hard way on my current trip to China.

As I said, a word like "orange" is pretty invaluable when you want to order a simple glass of orange juice.

The same is true in China, as I found out a couple of days ago on my recent business trip there.

While the primary Chinese dialect, Mandarin, is basically the same wherever you might speak it throughout the world, there are a few words spoken in China that are not really used by Chinese speakers anywhere else in the world.

Let me give you a couple of examples.

Anywhere else outside of China, when you refer to a waitress in a Chinese restaurant, you address her using the Chinese words, "Xiao Jie", which basically means "young lady."

However, in certain parts of China, I recently learned that you do not refer to a waitress in China with the term "Xiao Jie", because culturally, that term is usually reserved when you are addressing a um…well…a "lady of the night". Or how about a woman working in the oldest profession? I'm sure you know what I mean.

You might also be interested to know that the Chinese phrase for orange juice anywhere outside of China is "Ju-zi shwei", which literally means "orange water". However, ordering orange juice in China by using the phrase "Ju-zi shwei" will give you a blank stare from your server, because the phrase will sound like gibberish, as if you took the phrase "orange juice" and replaced it with a nonsensical word like, say, "putty-moo", because their word for orange juice is "chen jr", which is a word I had never heard.

I wish someone had told me this just a little bit sooner.

That's right, you guessed it. At my last breakfast in communist China, I nonchalantly flagged down my waitress, smiled, and proceeded to loudly and confidently blurt out the following request, in Chinese:

"Good morning prostitute! When you get a chance I would really like you to give me some putty-moo."

You would never have guessed that there were so many government police assigned to that restaurant that day.

The Seven Habits of Highly Effective Asians

Habit Number Five:
Shoes off or your feet off

After reading the book, "The Seven Habits of Highly Successful People" by Stephen Covey, it had such a profound impact on me that it inspired me to come up with my own list, this one specific for Asian Americans.

It is my sincere hope that the list I've come up with will provide some insight into the intricate workings of Asian socio-economic dynamics, some helpful hints on how to improve your own productivity, and perhaps most importantly, allow me to sell twelve kajillion books.

In the interests of full disclosure, let me first say that I am an Asian American, who is writing from a particular perspective. Therefore, the opinions that I am about to express may not necessarily represent the opinions of this publication. Having said that, if you do not believe in everything I am about to say, then your mama wears army boots and you are a complete chowderhead.

Now that I've gotten that out of the way, and without further ado, let me present the definitive list entitled, "The Seven Habits of Highly Effective Asians."

Habit Number One: *Rice – A staple as well as an adhesive*
While rice is a staple crop like potatoes and wheat, it is not widely known outside of the Asian culture that rice also serves as a be all, end all of adhesives. Go into any typical Asian home, and it is quite likely that you will not see any tape, glue, or paper clips. As most Asian kids learned at a young age, any time you asked your parents for some tape or glue for a project, they would eventually direct you to the refrigerator and a bowl of leftover rice. Take a few grains of day old rice, mash them together between your fingers, and Voila! Instant glue.

I recently helped my son build a treehouse using nothing more than some lumber, paint, and five bowls of leftover chicken fried rice.

Habit Number Two: *Banners – Not necessarily a sign of the times*
The next time you visit a Chinese, Vietnamese or other Asian restaurant, be sure to check out the restaurant sign out in front. More likely than not, you will see a "Grand Opening" banner hanging not too far from it. Asians realize that it makes no sense to invest hundreds of dollars on a "Grand Opening" sign only to use it for the first few weeks of a brand new restaurant. No, if it was a good idea to have the sign up for a few weeks, then it makes even more sense to have the signs up for the long haul.

When I was a kid growing up, I thought the name of my favorite Chinese restaurant was called "Beijing Gardens Grand Opening." It wasn't until a few years later that I started to get suspicious when the same restaurant changed its name to "Beijing Gardens Grand Opening Under New Management."

Habit Number Three: *Never judge a seat by its cover*

When invited over for dinner in an Asian household, you may notice upon sitting at the formal dining table that all the chairs have the thick, transparent plastic sheet covering the seat of the chair that came with the furniture when you bought it. You may also wonder whether your host may have inadvertently forgotten to remove the cover after they got the dining set home.

This is a common misperception by people who have not closely studied habit number three of the seven habits.

While most people assume the see through plastic covering is used only to protect the seat fabric while the furniture is in route from the furniture store to your home, it is a little known fact that this plastic material is an industrial grade product, manufactured to withstand liquid spills, sharp utensils, hot pans, and low grade nuclear explosions.

My aunt once proudly explained that her dining room seat covers were custom made using intricately hand woven silk from a rare silk worm that only lives in one nearly inaccessible area of China. She described the design of the seat covers in great detail, which she had to do by memory since you couldn't see anything through the faded, now yellow-colored plastic covering the seat.

But take my word for it – if anyone could see under the plastic I'm sure those seat covers would have been beautiful…and pristine.

Habit Number Four: *Tea'd off yet squeaky clean*
Habit Number Four is a daily ritual performed routinely on the lives of young Asian children throughout the world by their mothers. Asian mothers are convinced that tea is a magic elixir that will not only quench thirst, but is also a natural disinfectant that can clean anything known to man.

It's the same image the world over – an Asian mom holding a small towel in one hand and a pot of tea in another. Next thing you know, the tea is poured out onto the towel, and whatever the object – tabletop, chopsticks, 57 Chevy, is now clean.

Unfortunately, the object of my mom's disinfecting skills was often me and my brother. During the course of any meal you could predict that my mom would eventually pour hot tea onto a napkin and wipe our faces with it. While our faces would certainly end up clean, I'm not sure whether the tea was really effective or whether applying any liquid the temperature of scalding lava to a child's face would be a good disinfectant since it's likely to kill germs as well as burn off a few layers of the kid's epidermis.

I hope these habits will have a positive impact in your life. And for those of you who have noticed that I only got through four of the seven habits, hopefully you'll be able to find them in my upcoming book.

How else am I going to sell twelve kajillion copies?

Getting a Jump on the Competition, Unless You're Playing Checkers with Your Son

Checkers...the new Chess

A few nights ago my eight-year-old son Tyler came rushing to me with tears streaming down his face, sobbing uncontrollably, with the most broken hearted expression I've ever seen.

"What's wrong?" I asked, out of genuine paternal concern for an obviously traumatized and distraught young boy. Looking at his face, a rush of dramatic images flash in my mind. Who hurt my son? How did he get hurt? What do I need to do? Do we have any ice?

"Beth beat me in checkers!" he said, choking the words out in between sobs. Beth, by the way, is Tyler's nanny.

Still not quite understanding the situation completely, I began asking a few follow up questions.

"And then what?" I asked. "What happened after that?"
"Nothing. That's it!" he said, gasping for air.

"So what you're telling me..." I continued, "...is that the reason you're so completely beside yourself is because you lost a game of checkers. Beth didn't throw the board up in the air while celebrating and hit you in the head with it? She didn't scream 'Tyler is a loser!' and dance the chicken dance around you?"

"No" he said, sullenly, as if he had suddenly lost any reason for living.

"Then, the only reason for all of this is because you lost a game of checkers?" I repeated.

"But I beat almost all the kids at school!" he said, beseechingly.

As a responsible parent, I immediately ascertain that an earnest "father/son" talk is necessary. I spend the next few minutes explaining how important it is to be a good loser as well as a good winner, that he's only eight years old and he should know that he's at a distinct disadvantage when playing an adult because an adult has a lot more experience at checkers as well as life experience. I finish delivering my words of wisdom by telling my son that as he gets older, he will also improve at nearly everything, including checkers.

At the end of my little speech, we hug each other as only a father and son can, he wipes away his remaining tears, and goes off on his merry way.

A few minutes later, Tyler comes back – smiling, but this time, he's holding the checkerboard set in front of him.

"Ba Ba, would you play checkers with me?" he asks, very innocently.

As a responsible parent, I immediately ascertain that part two of the "father/son" talk is necessary. I agree to play, but I spend the next few minutes explaining that if we are going to play checkers, I am actually going to try and win. I explain that it does him no good for me to lose on purpose and that when I win, he needs to remember our earlier discussion about being a good loser. At the end of "Part Two" of my series of checkers playing etiquette, he nods his head in agreement.

OK…I think you know where I'm going with this.

We begin playing, and I take each turn – with one eye on the board and one eye on the TV. After all, it's OK to win but I should at least keep it close – he's still only eight years old.

I'm not sure when I realized I was about to lose this game. Maybe it was when Tyler started rushing me. "Hurry up, Ba Ba – what's taking you so long to move?" he'd say.

Maybe it was when I got up to turn off the TV and started to brew a cup of coffee. Maybe it was after I started responding to my wife by saying things like "Can't you see we're trying to play a game here?!?" every time she said it was time for Tyler to go to bed. Maybe it's when I shouted, "He can do his homework tomorrow!!!".

In the end, I accepted the situation, told him that he'd won, and carried him up to bed as he hugged me, as only a father and son can.

Needless to say, we played another round the following day, and this time with me carefully considering each move as well as frequently referring to the book "Checkers for Dummies", I ended up on top. Tyler, to his credit, took the loss well.

Now if my dad ever reads this, I know he's going to sit me down for part three of the "father/son" talk – only this time I'll be doing most of the listening.

Bless You, Yao Ming, Bless You

Made in China...
fed in America.

I used to be a rock star.

Strange though - except for the piano in my living room, I don't own a musical instrument. I've never fronted a rock band and I don't really sing in public. The closest I've come to singing in public recently was when I was driving my seven year old son from school the other day and singing to "Sweet Caroline" on the radio at the top of my lungs with the windows rolled down and a car load of kids roaring with laughter as we were both pulled up at a stoplight.

When will I ever learn? Windows down – play U2 or Eminem. Windows up and no one can hear you – Neil Diamond rocks!

OK, so in the strictest terms, I'm not an actual rock star. But I think I know what it feels like to be one – at least when I'm in China.

Here's how it works. In the U.S., I'm a fairly average-sized person. Six feet tall, average build, not too big, not too small.

When I go to China, especially in some of the more rural areas, that's another story. A six-foot tall Chinese man in China? I might as well wear a goose outfit carrying a sign saying, "I'm looking for duck-duck."

It starts up the moment I get off the plane. I have to duck under a lot of doorways. The seats are often too small. Walking up stairs, you often have to bend down so as not to hit your head on the ceiling. People walking pass stop in mid-stride with their eyes bulging and mouths agape, as if Big Foot had just disembarked from the plane.

At first I got kind of a kick from it. Waiting to board a busy subway, you're a foot taller than everyone else trying to board as you gaze over a sea of bobbing black heads. When I'm sitting on a bus, I usually get the bench all to myself because there's simply no room for anyone else on the bench once I sit down.

After a while though, you quickly discover that being overly tall in any country has a lot of drawbacks. I have to answer the same question every time. "What did your parent's feed you?" they ask, expecting me to say, "Oh, nothing special - hamburgers, hot dogs, human growth serum, the usual things."

Then, despite the fact that I have been to Asia countless times, I have yet to buy a single article of clothing. Oh, I've tried, but I can never find anything big enough for me to wear. I immediately start feeling like a sideshow geek. You can see the sales people sizing me up, with a look of bemused amazement when I walk into the store. You can hear them trying to figure it out, speaking Chinese, unaware that I understand what they're saying.

"Someone go in the back and see if we have any shoes that'll fit this guy. He's huge. See if we still have those clown shoes leftover from the party. Maybe those will fit."

It's enough to give you an inferiority complex. You start believing that perhaps, there really is something wrong with you. You get paranoid. You start questioning yourself.

Am I really that big? I seemed fine at home. Wait a minute. Why am I so tall? Why do I have all these bruises on my forehead from bumping into doorframes? Look at my hands. They're freakishly big! I could strangle a cow with these hands! I've got cow-killing hands!

Fortunately, I've recovered from my paranoia, thanks in large part, to the very large Yao Ming, center for the Houston Rockets basketball team, who ironically enough, is from China. He's seven feet, six inches tall, and I'm sure he really does know what it's like to be a rock star.

I just wonder what his parents fed him?

An Unexpected Gift

Sometimes you don't find out about the life of a man until that life is gone.

I lost a cousin last week. He was far too young to go. I knew him as a down to earth, unassuming, and good-humored person. I knew he liked to take pictures. I knew that if there were a family reunion, no matter what, cousin Horace would be there.

But most of what I knew of him I learned when we were both kids.

He loved gadgets and electronics. He loved music and comic books. He liked to fish, and the fish seemed to sense his joy by rewarding him with a lot of activity while my line would sit noticeably still in the water. At the time, he lived close to us and since he was a couple years younger, it often felt like I had a 2nd little brother when he was around.

Time goes on, and while he only lived about two hours away, except for our annual family reunions, life often takes you down separate paths. He stayed single while I got married and ended up with a carload of kids. Life moves on and before you know it, you start to lose touch.

Of course, when I found out that he had become gravely ill, like much of our extended family, we rushed to his side, in the hopes that he might just make it. Instead, each of us got to stand by him, and quietly say our goodbyes.

It wasn't until then, and in the following days, that I really got to know cousin Horace. I learned so much more about him. I learned his life was about so much more. I learned about how beloved he really was.

I learned all of this from his friends.

The moment we arrived in the hospital to see him, there were waves of people, crowding the waiting room, lined up along the hospital corridor, many sobbing, completely grief stricken. At one point there were 50 people, practically lined up down a hallway, waiting to get a chance to see Horace.

I spoke to many of them. Each one of them had a unique story to tell, describing in great detail how Horace had gone out of his way to help a friend or lend a shoulder to cry on. He would help friends who never asked for his help. He would surprise friends by dropping by to cook a fancy dinner or buy a welcome mat with a dog pictured on it because he knew his friend liked dogs.

I met one woman who told me that Horace had taught her to speak English when she came to the U.S. in the 1980's. Another friend sobbed as she told me that Horace had bought her a new car when she needed one. Two or three more friends explained how Horace helped them get through a tough divorce.

Horace would drop by unexpectedly at one workplace or another and volunteer to fix their computers or deliver some food. He would arrive for a party and serve as the unofficial photographer for the evening. In a casual conversation, if someone happened to mention that they needed a book, or stapler, or panty hose, Horace would go out of his way to get it for them.

One friend mentioned, "Horace always has a smile on his face. At the end of the day, that is the one thing you can count on – Horace is smiling."

The outpouring of love and support from Horace's huge network of friends was a surprise to many of us in the family. Not that anyone was surprised that he had friends, but mostly from the sheer magnitude of it.

I can't speak for anyone else, but my first reaction was a pang of guilt – I should have paid more attention. I should have made more of an effort. I should have known.

But such feelings can't change the past, and fortunately, my life has been full of blessings already. For cousin Horace - his life, at least according to his friends, was exceptionally happy.

Instead, I've come to the realization that while I could have had a closer relationship with Horace, I still have time to make a difference in the lives of all my other cousins and all my friends.

I have a handful of friends where I can recall one or both of us saying that while we rarely stay in touch, we both know that we are the best of friends and will remain so. Yet, ever so gradually, time has passed and I can barely remember the names of their children, or if they've moved on from a job recently.

Last year I got together with an old friend and didn't immediately recognize him as his hair had turned gray.

I know now, that a true friendship needs to be nurtured, just like anything you truly care about. What I've learned from Horace, in the way he lived his life, is that I need to be present in the lives of those I care for.

That is the unexpected gift Horace has given me, and I am just one more person who owes him debt of gratitude. Thank you so much, Horace.

I know, somewhere out there – Horace is smiling.

A Belt-Free Vacation

When does a craving become an addiction?

We all know that true addiction can be a life or death situation. With cravings, not so much. It only seems that way.

Case in point – our summer vacation in Vancouver.

Every summer, we spend a few weeks in Vancouver, Canada. It's a time to unwind, enjoy time with friends and family…and eat like it's going out of style.

Seeing as how Vancouver has a huge influx of people from Hong Kong, most of our meals revolve around Chinese food. For those who don't know about my family, when I use the phrase "revolve around", what I really mean is "consists entirely of".

I will be the first to admit my craving – steamed buns with black sesame seed paste. I know it doesn't sound like much but ohhhhh, even the thought of biting into one of these scrumptious little buns oozing with my version of black gold. Ahhhh…oooh…buns of mouthwatering goodness.

I know, it sounds oddly erotic but I don't know how else to describe it.

Calling my wife's love of dungeness crabs a craving is an understatement, and it doesn't matter how they are prepared. Steamed, stir fried, baked, or live out of an aquarium, she will take it any way she can get it.

Anyone who knows my wife Maya will tell you that she's a picture of sensibility, always a healthy eater, and always looking for nutritious foods that are both nutritious and flavorful. But put a platter of crabs in front of her and it's best to keep your hands to your sides and wear protective eyewear in case the remnants of flying crustacean debris are flung your way.

In fact, during our stay we spent two days crabbing off a local pier, but we didn't catch much. I don't know whether our lack of luck was due to it being late in the season for crabs or maybe all the crabs near the pier hightailed it for deeper waters every time a certain wild-eyed woman approached the pier wearing a bib and carrying a bowl of drawn butter.

Most interesting were the cravings of two of my best buddies, Victor and Vinh, who have lived in the U.S. most of their lives but grew up in Hong Kong and Vietnam, respectively.

Sure, being active types we had a terrific time biking around, hiking, going white water rafting, and generally seeing the sights, but what impressed me the most was when we went shopping for groceries in a local market and came upon the fruit section.

You could see each of them, stop in mid-stride, with their eyes wide open and mouths agape.

As one of my buddies started blubbering in some incoherent, oblivious way, I could faintly hear the other say something like, "Ohhh....Mama."

What they were both staring at were a variety of exotic fruits, some of which just aren't sold back home.

"They've got bon-bons here.", Victor said, in mid-blubber.
"And Mangosteens", Vinh said, after wiping away a bit of drool.

"Mangosteen and bon-bons?", I asked, feeling puzzled as I saw no evidence in this section of any cattle or chocolate truffles.

Apparently, both Victor and Vinh had come across a number of exotic fruits, many of which they had not had since they were seven or eight years old. I'd heard about how the scent or taste of something could trigger vivid memories of your childhood, but I had no idea of the magnitude of their reaction.

For the rest of the trip, our days would start early and our activities were planned based on our proximity to the nearest Asian supermarket for whatever bizarre produce we were after for the day.

"Psst...Wayne, wake up. We're going on a bon-bon run."

"What? We're going on a what? What are we going to do?"

"Get up. Victor and I are going to Kingsway Street to get some longans and some bon bons."

"Vinh, Kingsway is nearly an hour away. You do know that, right?"

"Good point. We're going to need some gas. Let's go."

Obviously, my friends were not sensing the silliness of their actions. For a moment, I thought I might try to talk some sense into my friends by explaining what a waste of time it was to drive an hour away just for some exotic fruits and that they were getting a little carried away.

I thought that if I reasoned with them, they would come to their senses and realize the folly of going on some wild bon-bon chase.

Then I realized that I was getting dangerously low on my black sesame seed bun stash and that we'd better get moving if we were going to get back before sundown.

Time Marches On, Unless You Uninvite Yourself

On any given day, life presents challenges. The key is in how you roll with the punches.

When things get you down, take a deep breath. Turn the other cheek. Take time to stop and smell the roses. Go to your happy place.

Even better - draw a nice, warm bath, light some scented candles, and for an extra touch, toss a handful of freshly picked lavender petals into the water to set the mood as you ease in to the perfumed, silky smooth water.

Ahhh…*gurgle, gurgle*…life is sweet.

If you keep yourself in the right frame of mind, you can handle anything life throws at you.

Last week, someone backed into my car as I was about to leave and slightly dented my fender. Sure, I could have been upset, but I'm sure he was in a hurry and obviously didn't do it on purpose. Then, a few days ago, I had lunch with a friend and the waitress brought me the wrong order – twice. Again, she didn't mean it and I'm sure she was just having an off day.

Yesterday, a colleague of mine cancelled a meeting that we've had to reschedule three times already. Well, I thought, I'm sure it must have been something really important.

I just think life is too short to get worked up from such minor distractions.

So, it was with my serene peace of mind that I went about my day today. I got up, dropped my son off to school, jogged a couple of miles, made a few phone calls, and then went out to the mailbox to retrieve the day's mail.

There, among the junk mail, bills, and letters, was an invitation for me to join…AARP. The American Association of RETIRED Persons.

point! Now it's match point! I won the winning point! Yahoo! Look at everyone pointing at me, they're saying, "You're the point master!" Now it's off to Wimbledon to win some more points!

I could go on, but I think you get my point.

You don't earn any points when you're working out in a gym (and just in case you think I missed it – brownie points don't count). Of course, the reason why I go to the gym is to stay in shape. It's just that the actual activities you partake in at the gym seem so unproductive.

You run around a circular track as long as you can only to end up exactly where you started. Running on a treadmill is even worse. You start from point A, and forty minutes later you arrive at point...well, actually, you never left point A. Some treadmills will actually tilt upwards during the routine so now you're panting just trying to catch your breath as you try to scale a Himalayan mountain traverse that leads nowhere.

At least when you're hiking up a mountain you have some sense of control. Picture someone (OK...me) who's on level ten on the treadmill, with the machine at a steep pitch, barely keeping up with the machine, when all of a sudden, without warning, you have an overwhelming urge to...sneeze.

It's like someone installed an ejection seat on my treadmill. One minute you're running on the treadmill, the next you're body-slamming the gym floor like a professional wrestler. And of course, let's not forget...I'm doing this all for my health.

Lifting weights is the toughest exercise for me. You spend an enormous amount of energy to lift a really heavy object into the air. There's no objective to lifting the weight except to put it back down on the floor so that you can do it again and again. Your mind knows why you're doing it but your body clearly doesn't understand. You can almost hear your body speaking to you.

I've been patient with you on these weights, but enough is enough. You are now beginning to experience severe muscle spasms up and down your arms and legs and this will continue until I've made myself perfectly clear. Unless someone is paying you to lift these weights, you will soon experi-

ence what it's like to visit Cramptown, USA.

When I travel to Asia, I do my best to keep up my exercise regimen. The problem is, everybody there apparently has the same mindset towards working out that I do. You don't see many people exercising, and I suspect the reason is that they eat healthier, and have more active lives than we do.

The few times I've tried going for a jog in Asia, you see all sorts of people staring in my direction. They're not really staring at me, mind you. They're looking directly behind me to see who might be chasing me.

The Benefits Of Being The Human Pretzel

Ohhmmm…Ohhmmm…

Excuse me, I was concentrating on a yoga pose.

The surprising thing is, even as a beginner, I do see the value of it. I think I always did. Everyone I've seen who does yoga seems so limber and at peace. My impression was always that yoga was terrific, as long as I wasn't the one doing it.

Not that I think there's anything really wrong with it. I think it's my own Neanderthal male perception of things. Yoga is primarily for women, while men are supposed to play basketball, football, and later in life, we take a set of clubs and knock a little white ball around a huge lawn while wearing funny looking shorts.

Actually, the only real problem I had with yoga was my valid belief that I wouldn't be able to do any of it.

You see, after 45 years of playing primarily football, basketball and tennis, my body is very tight. I have a limited range in my muscles that allows me to do the things I do on a daily basis. Sitting, standing – no problem. I can walk, reach for things, pull things toward me, and sit back down. These motions allow me to walk to the refrigerator, pull it open, reach for a submarine sandwich, and sit back down in front of my plasma television.

A few weeks ago, I purchased a few yoga DVDs for my wife Maya to help her relax and work on keeping her back limber since she sometimes gets a bit stressed. Thoroughly enjoying it, she persuaded me to give it a try. Talk about Karma.

So it should come as no surprise that my first few attempts have been, to say the least, a challenge. I'm sure you've heard, from people who have taken up a new sport, that they "seem to have used muscles they didn't know they had." My first reaction to yoga is that I've been able to cause pain in parts of my body where I've never experienced pain.

To give you an idea of how tight my muscles have become, the last time I was able to stand, bend over, and lay my hands flat to the floor was circa 1995. The last time I could bend my leg and bring my foot near my head in any position, the Berlin wall was still standing. Nobody had heard of the Internet yet. Cell phones were the size of a loaf of bread. *Yahoo* was something you said if you won the lottery. A television remote was basically yelling at my little brother to get up and manually change the channel. You get the picture.

I try my best to follow the trainer's instructions. *Push your hands out. Raise your right leg. Lift your left leg and cross it over your right leg. Breathe. Now lift your head up and turn it to the right. Open up your muscles.*

Although the trainer is on a DVD and cannot hear me, I still find it worthwhile to blurt out, "It is anatomically impossible to make that move. There must be some special effects or CGI on this DVD that lets this guy make that move. He's defying the laws of physics and gravity!"

I'm sure I say these things primarily to cover up the fact that I can't come anywhere close to stretching my muscles like this trainer can. On the other hand, I doubt that he can do the "Refrigerator and submarine sandwich maneuver" nearly as fast as me.

Monitoring your breathing seems to be an important part of yoga as well. I understand that regulating your breathing while going in and out of a yoga pose helps in letting go of the stress in your body as well as being aware of the muscles that expand and contract while you are breathing.

My problem is that in any pose that requires me to bend at my torso, I can't control my breathing because there is no remaining air in my body. I look around and the room looks like it's going dark. I had no idea that the gracefulness of yoga could make me pass out. Technically speaking, any sport that induces oxygen deprivation ought to be considered an extreme sport, wouldn't you say?

On the other hand, maybe it's just me.

The United Federation of Asian Perfect-ness

I am a superhero. I've always known there was something different about me but until recently I couldn't quite put my finger on it.

I made this startling discovery after reading an article on Asian stereotypes and why, according to the author, all stereotypes, whether good or bad, are offensive. I'm not sure I agree with his point considering how many of the stereotypes he mentioned were just so, gosh darn complimentary.

Let's do a quick run through of the stereotypes in question:

Asians are smart! Ok, yes...me.
Asians are born with PhD-level math skills! Umm hmm...me again.
Asians are hard working! Again...me.
Asians are humble! Stop already! You're embarrassing me!

The evidence is in. I am a superhero. I mean, who wouldn't want to have these traits?

But because I'm a superhero by virtue of my Asian-ness, that also means the other billion or so Asians in this world are my fellow superheroes.

In fact, with so many of us around, we have formed an alliance. We've put together a kind of brainiac superhero organization dedicated to the pursuit of solving all mathematical equations with one slide rule tied behind our backs. A crack squad of overachievers that can leap tall physics equations in a single bound, be faster than a speeding calculator, and more powerful than a supercomputer.

Look! Up at the Pi! It's a bird. It's a plane! It's Superasian!!!

We've already taken this to the next level - conventions, tupperware parties, the whole nine yards (or 8.2296 meters, in case you were wondering). We have an annual dinner and instead of a keynote speaker, we just pour out a box full of used vacuum cleaner parts, batteries, duct tape and other odds and ends on stage and see where our imagination leads us.

Last year I lost to Bonnie Yurimoto who won in the "Most Innovative" category, but I still say my hovercraft was way better.

All right, enough. Let me just take a moment to forcefully unstick the tongue placed firmly against my cheek and state, obviously, that I am being facetious.

In point of fact, I am a living, breathing example of an Asian that dispels most Asian stereotypes. I don't really fit most the positive ones or the negative ones for that matter.

My math skills are beyond embarrassing. I routinely go to the "15 items or less" counter at the supermarket with 17 or more items. When I use a calculator, I do each calculation twice because I don't trust my ability to type the right keys. I boast to my wife that I got a B+ in Advanced Calculus in college but I neglect to mention that I didn't understand it even when I was taking the class. If I recall, my calculus finals used a multiple-choice format and I was on a hot streak that day (*Let's see…I chose answer "B" last time so this time I'll go for a "D"…*).

I do work hard but that has less to do with being Asian and more to do with having three kids, one dog, a big mortgage, and a steady craving for Krispy Kreme donuts.

As far as whether I match up with negative Asian stereotypes, let's see. I'm six feet tall, have never owned a laundry, did not study to be an engineer, don't know what a pocket protector looks like, and I was a running back on my high school football team. And while my math skills have never taken me very far, I've always had a knack for writing.

None of that makes me super, but it suits me just fine.

Anniversary of Diminishing Returns

My wife and I recently celebrated our 17th wedding anniversary. The first few anniversaries were special events - a long weekend in wine country, his and her massages at an upscale spa, or a candlelit dinner in a French restaurant with a view of the ocean. Each year's milestone was further testament to the power of our wedded bliss, the strength of our relationship, and the realization that we had each found our one true love - a love worthy of an annual celebratory extravagance. Someone cue the violins.

As each year passes though, it's tough to keep up that level of enthusiasm and well, downright zeal. For example, our last anniversary was a bit more mundane. My wife Maya gave me a card, a generic card without any specific message on it from a set of cards she bought long ago at a closeout sale. I know this because I was with her when she bought it.

Yet, I can't claim that I did much better. I managed to pick up a bouquet of flowers from Costco that I bought at the last minute as I was checking out with my gallon tub of peanut butter, four dozen eggs, and five-pound bag of breaded chicken cutlets. I did buy a very romantic greeting card and managed to scrawl something sentimental down while waiting at a stoplight on my way home for our anniversary. Unfortunately, I had to throw away that first card, and turn back to buy another one, when I realized that in my haste, I had signed the card to my wife with the words, "Best Regards, Wayne Chan."

Still, I can say without question that this woman from Taiwan, who I have known for nearly half my life, who came to the U.S. 20 years ago and couldn't speak more than a few words of English, is the love of my life. Perhaps as the years go by, it gets a bit harder to come up with a present or idea that will truly surprise your spouse on your anniversary, and maybe because of that you sometimes end up not trying as hard.

Yet, while it might not seem as romantic, the more important point lies in how your better half fits in with what I call the "I can't imagine" rule. I can't imagine not being able to share my day with her. I can't imagine not waking up to her every day. I can't imagine not having her in my life.

What do you know...more true than ever.

Perhaps some of the gratification I have towards my marriage is due to the fact that it started off a little rocky.

I had known Maya for only nine months, but even then, I knew she was the one. So, being an old fashioned type, I knew I would need to propose to Maya as well as ask her parents for their blessing. But, there were a few problems. Number one: Her parents both lived in Taiwan. Number two: Neither of her parents spoke a word of English. Number three: Despite the fact that we had been together for nine months, Maya had scarcely mentioned a word about me to her parents (what that says about her feelings for me at the time will be the topic of a future column).

Despite these problems, I was confident I could weather them. So I proposed - and after she gave it some thought, said a little prayer, and forced me to get a blood test, undergo a routine credit check and a thorough vetting of whether I had any prior felony convictions - she accepted.

It was what happened next that completely threw me for a loop.

Unbeknownst to me, Maya's father had been sending polite requests to her daughter for her to come back to Taiwan. He felt that she had gotten enough out of the American experience, and that it was time for her to come back home and start her career.

However, in this last letter from her father, he was no longer suggesting that Maya go back - he was now demanding it. As luck would have it, Maya received the letter the day after she had accepted my proposal.

So now, my mission was to introduce myself to Maya's parents, ask them to give us their blessing, rebuff the whole idea of Maya going back home... and do it all over the phone *and in Chinese*.

If I recall, the first words (in Chinese) out of my future mother in law's mouth were, "DO...YOU...SPEAK...ANY...CHINESE"?

Fortunately, Maya had phonetically written a series of statements down on paper on how I would ask my future in laws for their blessings to marry their daughter. Obviously, I did a good enough job since we've been married for 17 years now.

That's not to say that we haven't had our share of problems. That's a part of married life too. As anyone who has a successful marriage can tell you, the first few years of married life are spent just trying to sort out the major issues – money, privacy, and the big kahuna – the other person's feelings.

We've had honest disagreements over money. We've had conflicts on how best to raise our kids. We've had to face deaths in the family. Most recently, we had to deal with a driver who lost control and drove into our backyard.

The funny thing is, after the ground rules are set, you spend less time arguing about really important issues, but just as much time on issues that don't warrant any attention at all. Case in point, a recent conversation I had with my wife Maya in the kitchen.

Maya: You didn't replace the bottled water in the fridge.
Wayne: There's still some water in the bottle.
Maya: No, I saw what you did – there was hardly anything in it already, and you only drank a little just so you wouldn't have to get a new bottle.
Wayne: I only drank a little because I was taking my vitamins, and I only needed a little.
Maya: Well, if you go get a glass of water for any reason, and you only leave that little for the next person, you're forcing that next person to go get a new water bottle just to get enough water.
Wayne: What if the next person only needs a little water like me, just so he could swallow some pills? In that case, I've left just the right amount.
Maya: That doesn't make any sense!
Wayne: I'll tell you what doesn't make any sense – since you must have been the one to get some water right before me, why did you leave so little instead of just drinking a little more so you could leave a full bottle of water for the next person?
Maya: Obviously, I didn't need to do that because look how little you needed to swallow your pills!

The ironic thing is, after a long, drawn out discussion like this, a nice refreshing glass of cold water would have been nice. But both of us would rather face the early stages of dehydration rather than give the other the satisfaction of seeing the other get another bottle of water.

So instead, I search the refrigerator for something else to drink besides the disputed water, until I finally come across a can of prune juice that has been sitting at the very back of the fridge for heaven knows how long.

I pull the lone beverage out from cold storage, trying to avoid seeing any kind of expiration date before I drink it, when, out of the blue, Maya says, "Wait a minute. I was saving that for me!"

Apologies For A Twenty Five Year Old Wedgie

It's never too late to make an apology. Still, 25 years is probably pushing it a little.

My cousin Roger came to visit me the other day. I hadn't seen him in a few years, but as always, it was great spending time with him. We got to catch up with each other and reminisce about the "good ole' days".

Except for Roger, the "good ole' days" weren't always that good, especially when we were together.

You see, Roger is seven years younger than me, which meant that when I was sixteen years old, Roger was nine. And as the older cousin, I took it as my job, dare I say, even my responsibility to tease and torment him at every possible opportunity.

Unfortunately for Roger, I was exceptionally good at my job.

I didn't do anything out of the ordinary, mind you. No, as I recall, it was just your boilerplate teasing, occasional wedgies, and to be sure, tickling always seemed to be involved.

While my memory of this period in our lives is pretty hazy, Roger apparently managed to mentally categorize every unflattering nickname, tickle, and humiliation that I ever unleashed on him.

What's perplexing is that I always thought that I was the "gentle" one. After all, I also had a younger brother, and Steve was three years younger than me but still four years older than Roger. As my baby brother, Steve was the first to withstand my pranks, and I think he took particular pleasure to finally be the tormentor instead of just the tormentee.

In fact, there were times where I stopped Steve from going overboard with Roger. I mean, it's one thing to pour a bit of vinegar in someone's mouth while he's sleeping. Adding a tablespoon of wasabi to it is just crossing the line.

For all of my fellow eldest siblings out there, we are all part of a club that recognizes the fine art of aggravating our younger siblings. Our intent was not to create pain. Discomfort? Yes. Public humiliation? Of course. But with many years of practicing and refining our craft, creating any kind of pain is not only unnecessary, it's downright unsophisticated.

Yes, I was the kind one.

Still, after all these years if Roger is still a bit distraught, I am big enough to offer a public apology.

Roger, for that time where I laid you on top of a blanket and rolled you up into a human burrito, please forgive me.

For that time I created the "Man" test and challenged you to keep both your arms up for a count of ten while I tickled you profusely under your arms in order for you to prove that you were a man, I apologize. I also regret taking about four minutes to count to ten.

For that time when you fell asleep on our recliner and I gently poured warm water all over the front of your shorts and waited for you to wake up so that I could feign shock and dismay – I am truly sorry.

Roger is now an adult and he turned out to be a terrific person, as I knew he would. And yet, when he came to visit and saw my ten year old son Tyler, Roger put his arm around Tyler and said, "Tyler, let me show you a few things." He then turned back to me and half jokingly said, "It's payback time."

So Tyler, my son – I'm afraid I owe you an apology too.

A Meat and No Potatoes Kind of Guy

It was a moment two months ago that I will never forget. I stood on the small digital scale in my office, staring at the readout, unable to comprehend the number that flashed in front of me. "That can't possibly be right", I thought to myself.

The next thought was – perhaps the scale needed to be recalibrated. The good news was that I was right – it did need to be recalibrated. The bad news was that with the correct calibration I now weighed two pounds more.

Getting desperate, I started looking around the scale wondering if any of my children or my dog Bingo was jumping on the scale behind me whenever I turned away. No children. No dogs. There was only an overwhelming feeling that I needed either to go on a diet or gain a few more pounds and look into sumo wrestling as a new profession.

Since that fateful day, I've lost about 20 pounds on the Atkins diet. Atkins, of course, is the diet that limits carbohydrates. I did some research on "The Zone Diet" and "The South Beach Diet", which are two other popular diets designed to help you lose weight as painlessly as possible. For those of you who are also interested in finding a diet that lets you "have your cake and lose it too", let me just save you some time – there's no such thing as the "Krispy Kreme Diet". Believe me, I've checked.

The Atkins diet claims that you can eat as much steak, eggs, and bacon as you want as long as you stay away from starchy foods (rice & bread, for example). I decided to test this theory out to the extreme for the first few days. I went to an all-you-can-eat establishment, holding a platter the size of a spare tire, layered from one edge to the other with steaks, chicken, hot dogs – anything protein related.

By the time I made my way back to the table, looking at my plate I thought, "That should be enough meat… if I were a bear getting ready to hibernate.

As an Asian, Atkins is hard to follow since I am addicted to noodles, rice and dumplings. I recently went to a Vietnamese Pho restaurant (beef noodle soup) where I proceeded to order a bowl of noodle soup minus the noodles. I've had lunch at a dumpling house where I shucked all the dumpling skins like they were peanut shells only to gorge myself on individual fillings. Do you know what it's like to try and tell a sushi chef that you'd like a California roll without the rice?

The real problem is my metabolism. A bowl of chicken broth can sustain me for a week and a half.

Yet, this really should be a blessing. It could be a product of evolution. Could it be that my slow metabolism is a centuries old response to my ancestors having to struggle in China with a minimum of resources and very little to eat? Perhaps I should be grateful that my ancestors have passed along the ability to survive in a sparse environment.

It's something to ponder over as I sit down to eat spaghetti and meatballs sans the spaghetti.

A Massage to Die For

I've been thinking about getting a new chair for my desk. I'm sitting here at my desk – writing – and thinking – I need a new chair for my desk. Nothing really wrong with the one I have, but after visiting a friend a while ago and seeing his state of the art desk chair with all it's mesh supports and hydraulic lifts, it's time for a new chair. Until now, I never knew that sitting in a chair without pneumatic back supports was akin to being stretched out over hot coals. How did I ever get through the day?

I'm not sure when it was that I became so attentive to my sitting needs. In fact, as I look around me, I never realized how much I've invested in accoutrements that provide the ultimate in comforts. My desk is right next to a window for fresh air, but if it ever gets stuffy, I have a fan. In fact, my office has two fans. Whenever it gets truly warm, I have a small air conditioning unit near my desk. On top of that, the office already has central heat and air conditioning, which makes you wonder why I really needed two fans and a separate air conditioner to begin with.

When did I first place an emphasis on having a cushy existence? Why do I only buy shoes without laces now so that I never have to go through the dreaded experience of tying shoe laces? Did I really need to buy a remote control that helps you find lost remote controls?

I suppose part of me says that I've worked hard in my life and I've earned a few creature comforts. Now that I've hit my middle age, I've reached a time in my life where I'm no longer concerned about other people's perceptions. I no longer worry about whether or not I'm a "man's man" and whether I can take a little heat.

That wasn't always the case, though. When I was a teen, I had something to prove. I was a 16 year old with a mission.

I remember a trip I took to Taiwan years ago, where I met up with my cousin who was a year younger than me and was studying Chinese there over the summer. One day, we met up with my uncle who was a very successful businessman in Taipei. He was what we hoped to be someday - successful, respected, and in the prime of his life. He decided to take us out for a night on the town.

After dinner, my uncle decided he would take us to a private club to have a few drinks (martini for him, soda for us) and to treat us to a professional massage. For a couple of teenage boys, this was the life we thought we wanted, and we were determined to enjoy it. Dinner, private club, a massage – all we needed was a couple of cigars, a chauffeur named "Gibson" and a toy dog to sit on our lap and our lives would be set.

As we both laid face down on two adjoining tables, two masseuses came in, and started working their magic on two teenage backs that clearly didn't deserve or need a massage. As they continued, the pressure from their hands became more and more pronounced to the point of being uncomfortable. Still, a little discomfort in the lap of luxury was nothing to complain about, and I certainly wasn't about to show any displeasure in front of my cousin, who seemed to be enjoying himself.

Our masseuses asked us if we were comfortable and if we wanted more pressure. My cousin immediately agreed, and not wanting to be shown up, I nodded for them to continue.

Our masseuses responded by climbing onto the massage table to walk on our backs. You might not think that a 110 pound masseuse walking on your back would be all that bad, but you would be wrong. Especially when your masseuse seems to be deliberately walking on your back on her heels.

By now, I was sweating profusely and having some trouble breathing. I glanced over at my cousin to detect any sense of discomfort from him. Even though his masseuse seemed a few pounds heavier than mine, he wasn't complaining, although our conversation seemed a bit labored.

"How are you feeeelinguhh..?" I asked, with the words being squeezed out of my body.
"Fineuhh...", he said.
"Can you take a little more pressure?" our masseuses asked.
"Absoluooootelyehhh" my cousin said.
"Go forrrittttuhh..." I responded, not wanting to let on that that I suspected one of my lungs had already collapsed.

In order to put more pressure into the massage, our masseuses kept walking on our backs but now, raised their arms, and pressed their hands against the ceiling to exert more force on our backs.

I felt my spleen moving from one side to another. I heard cracking sounds with each step but I wasn't sure if it was coming from the table or me. I wanted to scream but I couldn't draw a breath to make a sound. I wondered whether the masseuses were trained in CPR and I started thinking about how much I missed my mommy.

The massage ended thankfully, with both of us relatively intact. Five minutes later, my cousin said, "Wow, to tell you the truth, I was dying but I didn't want to say anything in front of you."

So you see, my new chair really does need pneumatic back supports.

The Britney and Beijing Accord

It turns out that the fashion police are alive and well in China, and they have set their sights on Britney Spears.

Pop star Britney Spears is scheduled to give a number of concerts in China next year, but in light of the recent furor over Janet Jackson's breast baring performance at this year's Super Bowl, China's cultural officials have taken great care to eliminate any potential "wardrobe malfunctions" during her appearances. As a start, they have demanded to get a first look at her performance and her wardrobe.

According to one official, "Every aspect of her tour will have to undergo examination and approval. That especially goes for the clothes she'll be wearing. The requirement is that they don't show too much."

As a Chinese-American who would like to contribute whatever I can to ensure a positive relationship between the U.S. and China, I have taken it upon myself to draft a set of standards that might help address the situation. It is called "The Britney and Beijing Accord."

#1   Chinese cultural officials must approve all song lyrics in advance of the performance. However as a general rule, songs pertaining to anything of a sexual nature are prohibited. Songs addressing topics like the weather, beautiful scenery, fresh fruit, or China's entry to the World Trade Organization are generally acceptable.

#2   Songs featuring androgynous, half dressed male dancers moving provocatively on stage are prohibited. However, having government officials standing at the back of the stage clapping in unison is acceptable.

#3   Dancers should refrain from grabbing any other part of their body during the performance. If a "body part grab" is an intrinsic component of a particular song or dance routine, performers should restrict their grabbing to areas such as their head, shoulders, knees, and toes. As a side note, one fully acceptable maneuver is if the performer should choose to place both hands on their knees and bring their knees together repeatedly while simultaneously crossing their hands to the opposite knee. This is formally known as the "Hey, look what I'm doing with my knees!" routine.

#4   Removal of any article of clothing by oneself or by another performer (outside of a hat) is strictly prohibited. Stage managers reserve the right to apply super glue to any article of clothing should said clothing appear to be nothing more than a prop.

#5   Suggestive words in otherwise acceptable songs must be altered for the performance. The word "baby" should be replaced with the word "infant." The word "lover" should be replaced by "husband" or "wife", and the word "fondle" should be replaced with "look". Use of the word "loin" can only be used for songs addressing cuts of meat. Likewise, words like "ache" or "throbbing" are to be used only for songs recounting a recent sports injury.

#6   Stage costumes must conceal every inch of skin below the chin. Chinese formal silk qipao's are acceptable, full-length body armor is not only acceptable but encouraged.

The trouble is, after following all of these guidelines, Britney's show might only run for 20 minutes.

Would You Like That with a Side of Grits or an Egg Roll?

If you ever want to get a real sense of how diverse various cultures can be, don't bother going to New York, San Francisco, San Diego, Seattle or Los Angeles. To truly get an education, go to Belmont, Mississippi.

Don't get me wrong. I love the sights and sounds of the big city. I love that in most big cities you can go from a Japanese tea garden one moment, and walk a couple blocks away to have a Chicago style hot dog from a cart or visit a Turkish Hookah cafe across the street. By the way, if a tourist from Indiana named Henry Henderson regularly visited a Turkish Hookah café in Texas, would it be proper to say that Hoosier Henry Henderson was hooked on a Houston Hookah?

Sorry, I couldn't resist. Anyways, back to my point.

The point is, what the big city provides in the way of variety and well, downright fun, can sometimes lack in the way of perspective. Contrary to what you see in the big city, that kind of variety is the exception, not the rule.

Which brings me back to Belmont, Mississippi. A couple of weeks ago I traveled to Belmont to visit with a client of mine who does a lot of business in Asia. Upon meeting Rusty (I'm going to call him "Rusty", just in case this column gets into the hands of a local Belmontian), I was surprised to discover that despite doing a lot of business in Asia, Rusty had never traveled there. In fact, the furthest point east that Rusty had traveled was Atlanta.

The meeting was very productive, so much so that Rusty invited me to his favorite (and as far as I could tell, the only) Chinese restaurant in Belmont. Without mentioning any names, I'm just going to call it Rusty's Chinese Restaurant. Seeing as how I wanted to keep my client happy, I put my best game face on and readily accepted his invitation.

Upon arriving at Rusty's Chinese Restaurant, I discovered that it was an all you can eat establishment, which is not unlike many Chinese restaurants in the U.S. not located in a Chinatown or Asian business district.

I've always wondered why so many Chinese restaurants serve all you can eat buffets. Obviously, there's a market for it. But, why only Chinese restaurants? Why don't you ever see all you can eat Kabob restaurants, or a French-themed buffet serving big troughs of escargot, truffles and pate?

Despite Rusty's encouragement to try the buffet, I opted for their daily special. Now, I would be happy to tell you what the daily special was that day, but the description wasn't very descriptive and it still wasn't too clear to me even after my entrée arrived.

"Excuse me," I asked. "I was wondering, what is this?" (Spoken with an emphasis on the word "is")
"That's our daily special, darlin'" she said.
"Oh, I see…and what was the daily special again?" I asked, hoping for some additional clarification.
"Chicken Egg Foo Young" she said.
Finally, I pointed at a plastic container of thick, brown, somewhat lumpy liquid, and asked, "…and how should I use this?"
"Well sweetie, whatcha got there is your sausage gravy for your chicken egg foo young."

Now, I have had the good fortune of being able to travel to Asia for business quite often, and my culinary experiences have run the gamut. I've eaten braised pigeon, deep fried rattlesnake, quail meatballs, and some seafood I've never even seen in aquariums. Yet in all my travels, I have never had chicken egg foo young with brown sausage gravy on it.

But you know what? I liked it. It was warm, filling, and seemed homemade. In the end, you can't ask for anything more than that.

Despite all my travels, it was in Belmont Mississippi where I discovered that culture inevitably adapts to its environment. When facing a new environment, that would probably be a good idea for all of us as well.

Of course, the unanswered question: What did my chicken egg foo young taste like? Yes, yes – it tasted like chicken.

Inner Peace – Yes, Outer Silence – No Way

You reach a point in your life where you begin to ask often-unanswerable questions: What is the meaning of life? Who is watching over us? Are we alone in the universe? Why does an ice cream store scooper always hand you the ice cream cone first **before** asking you to pay which requires you to perform a complex juggling maneuver in order to get your wallet out and hand them money without dropping your ice cream?

Such are the unknowns we must all ponder.

Self-discovery can come in many different forms. For some, practicing yoga has helped people find an inner peace. Others have chosen to lead a simpler life, sometimes to the point of selling all of their worldly belongings in order to live a less complicated existence. It seems to me the common thread that weaves through every act of self-discovery is the search for an answer to the inevitable question – Is this all there is?

So when my wife suggested that we attend a meditation retreat at a local Buddhist temple, far be it for me to say no. This was to be a daylong gathering of people sharing the goal of rediscovering ourselves, leading perhaps to a better understanding of our spirituality. Not a bad time for a diet either, with all the vegetarian food being served.

As the day began, we were first introduced to the act of "mindfulness". My understanding of "mindfulness" is quite simple. It means, as I've read, "being aware of your present moment." As we practiced mindfulness throughout the day, the intent was to notice the subtle changes of our bodies as we meditated, understanding how we can control our pattern of breathing, and how we relax or contract the muscles in our body.

Mindfulness, almost by definition, also means that you must be silent. Not a word is to be uttered. It makes sense, for after all, how can you be aware of your present moment when you're busy talking to someone else, distracting them from discovering their present moment?

I found the necessity of having complete silence a real benefit to the entire experience. I am, by any account, an introvert. If not for necessity, I could go on for days without speaking to anyone. For the first time in my life, I was in an environment that not only encouraged but in fact, demanded my own inclination for anti-social behavior.

It was a different experience for my wife Maya, though. When Maya walks into a room, she is usually the center of attention. She is the life of the party. She makes her living by speaking to others as a management consultant, sometimes one on one, sometimes to hundreds of people.

As the retreat began, it soon became apparent that this whole "no talking" business was going to become a problem. About every other minute, as I was reveling in the silence, Maya would whisper something like, "Isn't this temple beautiful?" or "I wonder if they'll be serving tofu for lunch?" Each time, as if to underscore the point, I would shush her and quietly say, "Mindfulness."

As the day wore on, the frustration grew.
"I wonder where the bathroom is?"
"Shh…mindfulness."
"Where's the cell phone?"
"Ahem…mindfulness."
"Well, how am I supposed to…?"
"Tsk, tsk…M.F.N!!!"

The day ended, only two hours after it started, when the following words were spoken within earshot of everyone attending: "That's it! I'm outta here!"

Well, I suppose we can always give yoga a try.

Coming Soon – Casa de Vietnam

By any measure, the United States represents the perfect notion of living in a "melting pot". Where I live, the idea of living in a region where cultures co-exist and even coalesce becomes almost an afterthought at times. I have always been a believer that diversity enriches people. When it comes to food, I can't think of an easier way to experience the delights of a different culture.

I live in a city where you can try a different cuisine every night of the year and not run out of new adventures. Portuguese one night, Persian the next. How about Italian? But do you want Northern Italian or Southern, or how about getting even more specific with Sicilian? Twenty-five years ago, going out for Chinese meant a choice of perhaps three restaurants, one of them was purely for Chop Suey and the other two were basic variations of Cantonese food. Now, you have Szechwan, Hakka, Hong Kong seafood style, Vietnamese-Chinese, those specializing in hot pots, and many, many more.

But even the best intentions can sometimes go too far. Or maybe I'm more conservative than I thought I was.

I'm referring to a relatively "new" cuisine called **Fusion**. It may also sometimes be called **Pan Asian** or **California** cuisine.

My best guess as to the origins of this cuisine is that it started when a restaurateur was brainstorming new ideas for a restaurant, but was hard pressed to come up with a truly innovative idea that had not been done before. At some point, he must have thought, "Sure, you can have Japanese food one night, Cajun food the next, and Italian the night after that, but what if you could sample seven or eight cuisines, all from the same entrée?"

All of a sudden, entrée ideas come out from nowhere, nouveau chefs sprout flamboyant new creations and the world is full of possibilities. Excuse me, make that the **balsamic vinegar infused-world** is full of possibilities.

Here are a few entrees I pulled off from a local fusion restaurant I visited recently:

1. **Ancho-sesame BBQ Free Range Chicken** – Anchovy barbeque sauce, wild rice with currants, apples & walnuts topped off with a wild watermelon-jicama-lime salsa.

2. **Shaved Grana Salad** – Sardine filets over romaine lettuce with lime pepita dressing, sesame bread sticks, and red tortilla strips & roasted pepitas along with chile-fennel mahi, prawns or chicken.

3. **Air-dried Roasted Duck** - roasted air-dried Virginia wild duck served with a ginger-cherry sauce and a mixture of wild and basmati rice

4. **Good Things Growing** – Eggplant & roasted bell roulades, garam masala butternut squash ravioli & tempura yams with nut crusted tofu.

The last entrée stated that "A portion of the profit from this dish will go to benefit the Humane Society."

I wonder why they reserve so much compassion for the animals yet spare no mercy when it comes their meals?

As for what I ordered that night, I looked long and hard for an entrée with ingredients that I could actually identify. I settled for duck-filled dumplings in some sort of broth. I like duck. I like dumplings. Who doesn't like broth?

What I ended up getting was a dish covered with deep fried green onions and some other vegetation I couldn't identify that covered the entire bowl like a marsh from the Florida everglades. Once I hacked through the brush, I came upon the dumpling soup I ordered. Although I was somewhat put off by the fact that there were only three dumplings in the broth (which comes out to be about four dollars a dumpling), after my first bite I realized that the scarcity of dumplings was more of a blessing in disguise.

Of course, tasting the dumpling becomes a challenge when it is drenched in the soup itself.

It was like drinking a bowl of boiled honey. It was tooth achingly sweet. I didn't know whether to drink it or pour it over some ice cream.

It took hundreds, if not thousands of years for some cultures to establish the unique flavors and ingredients of their cuisine. All of this tradition and custom is now vulnerable to the "Hey, let's try this!" philosophy of Fusion cuisine.

I reject mango rumulade on my steak. "Infusion" is a medical term, not a culinary one. I don't know what ingredient "garam" is, and I don't want to find out. Tofu should not be on a pizza.

This is culinary creativity run amuck. Something must be done before someone starts making Portuguese sausage flavored gelato or fudge brownie clam chowder – with balsamic vinegar, of course.

Mother Nature Calls...
For Gloves And Goggles

Ahh...Mother Nature. To be in the element, to hear the sweet sounds of outdoorsy goodness – there's just nothing like it.

I see the trees, swaying gently with the wind as fall takes hold and turns all the leaves into vibrant hues of yellow and red. I pass by a creek, with water gurgling over smooth stones as it winds here and there on it's inexorable path to the ocean. I love nature.

Holy pinecones! I nearly ran over a possum. I'd better keep my eyes on the road.

There you have it, my friends. In just a few short sentences, I've managed to encapsulate my experiences in the wild. I've always loved the outdoors... from a distance.

So, it may come as a surprise to you that I've recently had a revelation. I've decided that man was not meant to be cooped up in a house, breathing recirculated air, constantly bombarded by the beeping of microwave ovens, or the buzzing of cell phones.

It dawned on me that while I have traveled the world from sea to sea, from New York to Shanghai, I have spent nary a day in my own backyard, which is the American west.

Well, that fact is about to change – American west – here I come!

But how? How about camping? No, not yet. I need to ease in to it. No need to jump in the deep end right away.

Stay at a hotel? Not enough of a stretch. How can you experience the outdoors from the confines of a hotel room? I can do better than that.

How does one experience the outdoors without having to brave the elements in a tent but not chicken out by staying in a cushy hotel?

Two words – Recreational Vehicle. Yup, the Chan family is going on an RV vacation! Woo hoo! Yippee! Someone alert the media!

At the time, it made perfect sense. I already know how to drive and the kids will love traveling in a house on wheels.

The only one I had to convince was my wife Maya. She was definitely not with the program.

If I recall her first reaction was, "Now I have to cook in a car? I don't want to cook in a car!"

I tried to convince her any way I could. I tried to explain.

"Look, sweetie, this is going to be great. It's so much more affordable than staying at a hotel. We don't have to move luggage back and forth. If we want to go somewhere, we just drive and everything goes with us!"

I think her response was, "I don't want to wash dishes in a car!"

Yet, the more she was opposed to the idea, the more I became obsessed with it. I started shopping for an RV, imagining month long trips all over the west. Hiking up the Rocky Mountains, traversing streams while fly fishing at the mighty Big Foot (yes, I saw that movie), hunting wild boar while camouflaged in a mixture of turkey feathers, leaves, and unscented deer dung – whatever it was, I was ready for it.

But before I got in too deep, a friend of mine suggested, "Before you buy any deer dung, maybe you should try renting an RV and see if you like it."

This made sense. If I could get Maya to enjoy her trip in a rented RV, then buying one would be the next logical step. I just needed to take care of all the details, so that she would enjoy herself.

So on one fateful day not long ago, we packed up, loaded up our SUV, and drove over to the RV rental place. I had watched the orientation video earlier and met with the rental specialist who walked me through the RV. I was ready to go.

First, I had to unload our luggage from the SUV. Then, reload it in the RV. Then we had to buy groceries and fit a weeks worth of food into a refrigerator the size of a large backpack. Once we got to our destination, I had to refill the tank with gas, and decided that as long as I didn't eat lunch for the next three months, I could afford it.

Once we found our spot at the RV park, there was another round of tasks to do. The RV had slideouts (portions of the RV that slide out to provide more room inside), which were easy enough to figure out. Then, hooking up the power and cable were pretty straightforward as well.

Which leads me to what, in the parlance of the RV world, are called, "cleanouts". In my entire life, I have never thought as much about what happens when you flush the toilet as I have on this RV trip. Of course, I realized that it had to go somewhere, but for the first time, I became an essential participant in ensuring that everything goes where it is supposed to go.

I had watched the video, and while it wasn't the most pleasant of all my tasks, it was arguably the most important. The video seemed pretty straightforward. It never occurred to me that we would be arriving at the RV park at midnight, and that I would have to perform this task for the first time in the dark. Unfortunately, asking my family to "hold it" for 12 hours seemed unlikely.

As I got outside to start, another RV owner spotted me and watched curiously as I stared into the cleanout tubes, trying to figure out what to do.

He said, "Excuse me, but you should probably put on your rubber gloves and goggles before you do that."

I looked around. Did this thing come with rubber gloves or goggles? Answer: No and No.

For the rest of the week, the only thing I could think of was, "This wasn't in the video."

Still, I managed to put it together and the rest of the trip was fine. The kids were having a blast, Maya managed to "cook in the car", and I took care of every last detail. Maya and the family had a great time.

At the end of the trip, I had to unpack the RV, load it back to the SUV, clean the RV inside and out, and dispose of all the trash we had accumulated. By the time I was done with this trip, I was ready for another vacation.

Last week, as we were trying to decide what to do for our upcoming winter vacation, Maya said, "Hey, why don't we rent the RV again?"

Does anyone have the toll free number to the Marriott?

How Not To Become My Own Zipcode

A recent study published in a British medical journal reports that over the last 10 years, the rate of overweight or obese people in China has exploded. According to the report, two out of every 10 people living in China would now be considered overweight or obese.

Of course, it should come as no surprise that here in the United States, the rates of obesity are even more prevalent.

In fact, latest reports show that six out of every 10 U.S. citizens have recently competed in the Pillsbury Doughboy Lookalike contest.

While the sedentary lifestyle and fast food culture of the U.S. are obvious culprits in our (literally) growing problem, finding the cause in China isn't nearly as clear. After all, China and the U.S. have very different cultures, and a major metropolitan Chinese city like Shanghai looks and operates nothing like, say – Los Angeles. Except for the recent explosion of people driving cars and the multitude of McDonalds and KFC's popping up on each street corner, the people in Shanghai should have no more reason to be overweight than…wait a second.

From a personal standpoint, my own struggle with keeping my weight down just took another hit. I can no longer rely on the rationalization that my lean and mean Chinese heritage will somehow miraculously neutralize the Big Mac or cheese filled crust personal pan pizza I had for lunch yesterday.

Therefore, for my own benefit, and for any of my readers out there who could use a helpful list of sensible eating habits, I have culled together the following list, which I call:

How not to become my own zip code:

#10. From now on, there is only one lunch per day. This is no such thing as a mid-morning lunch or an early afternoon lunch. The only time there should be two lunches in one day is if your first lunch consisted of a glass of water and seasoned ice cubes.

#9. A salad consists of lettuce, tomatoes, dressing, and a few croutons. If there happens to be a steak sitting on top of the salad, it is no longer considered a salad. It has now defined as a giant steakburger without the bun, and you are no longer allowed to eat it.

#8. An all you can eat restaurant should be considered a nice way to sample a variety of foods. It should not be looked at as a personal challenge.

#7. When ordering dumplings in a Chinese restaurant, if you've ordered so many dumplings that the kitchen staff calls in reinforcements to wrap more dumplings, you've ordered too many dumplings.

#6. If your favorite bar has a happy hour every night with fifty-cent tacos and you've already spent five dollars, you've ordered too many tacos.

#5. If your spouse catches you eating cheesecake as a late night snack, refrain from using the excuse, "Yes, but I'm drinking a glass of skim milk with it." Such a response will not only not work, it tends to make the situation even worse.

#4. When eating ribs, if the discarded bones on your table begin to look more like a paleontology excavation site, you've eaten too many ribs.

#3. The fact that Baskin Robbins has 31 flavors of ice cream should be appreciated for providing a nice range of choices. It should not be looked at as a personal challenge.

#2. Phrases such as "high in fiber", "lean", and "fresh" are descriptions usually associated with foods you should eat. On the other hand, phrases such as "stick to your ribs", "hearty", and "extra glob of gooey goodness" are usually associated with foods to avoid.

#1. When shopping for groceries, be sure to read the list of ingredients on the back of every item. If you need the scientific chart of the elements that you learned in junior high to decipher all the ingredients in the item (ie. Fructose, bicarbonate moxithion, the scientific symbol for magnesium, etc.), better to put the item down and find something else to eat.

Bruce Lee or James Bond – That is the Question

As an Asian American boy growing up in the 70's, I spent an inordinate amount of time weighing the pros and cons of both men. Most people watching a ten-year-old boy while his time away daydreaming about kung fu masters and super secret British spies might naturally assume the boy was placing his heroes into mortal danger in some adventurous exploit.

They would be wrong. In my mind, these were not fantasies. These were career options.

But, how to choose? How could anyone not want to be able to completely disable a dozen bad guys using just your feet, hands, and an ominous stare? On the other hand, how could anyone resist a tuxedo wearing secret spy who could shoot missiles out of his car or bust out of prison using a bomb set off by a watch/detonator thingamajig.

The biggest sell was trying to convince my parents. If I recall, through all of "discussion" (if you can call it that), I kept hearing the words, "doctor" or "lawyer" bandied about a lot.

Fine, I thought – just show me a doctor who can remove tonsils wielding a laser imbedded scalpel or a lawyer who gets to have his way with the defendants at the end of the trial and we've got a deal.

At ten years old, you haven't yet learned the word, "impractical". A ten year old never wonders why 20 bad guys surrounding Bruce Lee will politely wait their turn to fight Bruce individually instead of gang tackling him, which would seem to make more sense. Likewise, while Bruce Lee at a minimum suffers a few cuts and bruises and always manages to have his shirt torn off his body, a ten year old never questions why James Bond can fly his boat through a building, have his body ejected from an exploding car and fall from a ten foot building yet manage not to ruffle his hair or crease his still crisp tuxedo.

After all, these are exactly the reasons why I wanted to be like them.

I would love to impart some cultural wisdom on how my being an Asian American led me to face some questions of my own sense of identity as I struggled to parse out my feelings for the very western James Bond and the very Chinese Bruce Lee. I'd love to say that the time I spent dreaming about my two idols helped me better understand the two cultures in my life and that I've been able to help my kids as they are growing up.

I'd love to, but I can't. Come on - Bruce Lee had numchuks and James Bond drove an Aston Martin! What else do you need?

Yesterday, my son Tyler said he came up with his own superhero. He's nearly ten years old now, and he said that he was getting tired of the superheroes he's been following – Superman, Batman, & Spiderman. He calls his superhero, the "Shadowgripper", a dark and mysterious hero whose special power is the ability to "grab" shadows and turn them into objects he can use and shape at will.

Grabbing shadows? Kind of makes my thoughts of numchuks and laser watches seem a little underwhelming. Well, I should let him have his fun.

I'll even wait a few months before I start mentioning the words "doctor" or "lawyer".

A General's Generational Tale

A Chan family picture with General Chen Ji Tang seated in front, and my father, Shu-Yun Chan standing directly over his father's right shoulder.

Between 1928-1936, General Chen Ji Tang was the supreme ruler of southern China. He was a leader in the ruling Nationalist party at the time, and was a rival to the party leader, Chiang Kai-Shek. General Chen wielded enormous economic and military power in the region, and was commonly known as the "King of the Southern Skies" due to his military might.

I bring up this somewhat arcane fact not because I'm particularly interested in this period of Chinese history, nor to relate this to some facet of China's position in the world today. Instead, I sometimes reflect upon his life and times in a very personal way, as a contrast to my own life. You see, General Chen was my grandfather.

He lived and led during a tumultuous time in his country's history, when decisions had life and death consequences. At times he led his military to fight the Japanese invasion of China, and at times he fought against the emerging Communist movement, which would ultimately lead to the retreat of the Nationalist party, pulling back to the island of Taiwan.

Growing up, whenever my father's family would get together for a reunion, grandfather's exploits on and off the battlefield were often the topic of discussion. While many of the stories were undoubtedly true, I suspect through the haze of time that his legend in the family has only grown.

I have heard stories on how he single handedly led the way to modernize Southern China's infrastructure. I've heard that during the tumult of World War II, he received requests from the leaders of both sides of the war to recruit his support for their efforts. He is said to have traveled in a bullet proof car which he acquired after machine gun fire was sprayed all along his previous vehicle while he was in transit. I've been told that at a particularly dangerous period, grandfather would have his aides frisk his own children before allowing them to come into the house in case one of his enemies had successfully turned one of his own against him.

Yet even with the enormity of the times, it's the few personal anecdotes my father tells that stand out most in my mind. By all accounts, my father was not the favorite of grandfather. Caught up in the drama of his times, along with having 15 + other children among his three consecutive wives, grandfather could be dismissive, distant, blunt, and bad tempered to his children, and particularly with my father.

My dad was a sickly child, constantly in and out of the hospital, and his condition in the eyes of his father was often in stark contrast to the vitality, ambition, and spirit of his closest older brother, who happened to be the favorite of the family. I'm sure this is one of the reasons why my father does not often speak of his childhood.

In the few times my dad has spoken of his past, his life was often at odds with a family of tremendous wealth and power. His living quarters were in a separate building from the main residence, where his parents and his favored siblings lived. His room was sparse, with a cold, concrete floor, furnished with a hard, uncomfortable chair and a bed with very little padding. He was often scolded for being sick, and because his illnesses affected his schooling, his grades suffered as well, which would only bring more scorn and ridicule from grandfather.

The piano was a refuge for my father, a way of escaping the starkness of his life, enabling him to revel in the beauty and peace of Mozart and Beethoven's music. Unfortunately, grandfather often berated him mercilessly for playing the piano too loudly while he was trying to work or nap. He stopped playing shortly after that, and it was only a couple of years ago that he started playing again. I suspect that may be a reason why dad always pushed me to learn the piano.

With all this, it's one brief encounter between my father and grandfather that is the most vivid to me. As I recall, my father, a slightly built eight or nine year old, was just berated by one of the servants of the residence. He sat, alone, on a wood bench, looking forlornly and glum at the floor.

Grandfather, entering the room, sees his son, sitting alone, and decides to sit alongside his dejected son.

Quietly, and very tenderly, Grandfather raised his son's small and slender hand into the air, and placed his own open hand against the palm of his son. He looks down, into the eyes of his son, and says, "Everything will be alright. You see? Your hand is much smaller than mine but it is the same. You are a part of me." This is my dad's favorite childhood memory.

Dad passed away last year. My grandfather passed away long before I arrived. I wonder how he would have fared in today's world, where our greatest struggle of the day is often just getting through the daily commute without spilling hot coffee in the car. I wonder how I would have fared during the tumult of his times. I suppose these are questions that were never meant to be answered.

In the end, you live your life the best you can in the times you are in. The important thing is to honor your past, and to do your best to live up to it.

These two men – they are a part of me as well.

Watch Your Language; It May Save You (Asia Trip - Part One)

In order to give my current business trip to Asia the attention it deserves, this report will be the first in a two-part series chronicling my travels. Mostly though, I just like using the words, "Two-part series" and "chronicling".

First, a word about my credentials as a traveler to Asia - I don't really have any. Actually, I speak enough Chinese to help get me by when I'm traveling through China, Taiwan, Hong Kong, and when I'm shopping at the 99 Supermarket in Kearny Mesa.

The problem is, when people in China first hear that I can speak some Chinese, the rest of our conversation, no matter how complex the subject matter, is done in Chinese. When I'm trying to negotiate a business transaction, I don't know whether my comment "I hope we can make this business a 'win-win' situation" really came out as "My shoe is in love with the broken toaster." This can get you into trouble.

When I'm with a client in Asia, in order to impress them I must give them the perception that I know what I'm doing. Whether that is actually the case is beside the point. I need to keep up appearances.

While I speak some Chinese, I cannot read it. And yet, when we are at a business lunch, the waiter always gives me a menu completely in Chinese. In order to build up my reputation to my clients as *"Wayne Chan – savvy world traveler"*, I nonchalantly order items off the menu as if I know what they are. As I recall, the last lunch where I ordered off the menu consisted of three pots of tea, eight bowls of steamed rice, and 40 take out boxes of mushu.

A good rule of thumb when visiting Asia with only a partial command of the language is to keep things simple. Don't make special requests. It causes more grief than it's worth.

I once checked into a hotel and asked for a room with two double beds and a view of the ocean, close to my client. With my Chinese, the request sounded more like this:

I want…in room that I am paying to sleep in…please make me two sleeping furniture…then stand up see water way over there with other person too.

When I travel to countries like Malaysia and Thailand, I sometimes use a handy little translation program on my handheld computer. I recall one dinner at a Thai restaurant in Thailand (actually, wouldn't all restaurants in Thailand be called a Thai restaurant?) where I was particularly interested in a red curry dish. When the waiter asked me how spicy I would like it, I used my handy dandy translator to find the word, "mild". But after tasting the dish, I may have inadvertently substituted the word "mild" for the phrase "brain hemorrhaging-level spicy."

Take my advice – when in China, make generous use of the phrase, "Wu swo wei" (It doesn't matter). You'll be surprised how often it works.

Unaccustomed to Customs Checkpoints (Asia Trip - Part Two)

It seems every time that I cross the border from Hong Kong to China, a customs agent gets flagged by the computer that I am a suspected criminal. That is to say, someone by the name of "Wayne Chan" is a suspected criminal.

Each time I reach customs, they seem to go deeper and deeper into their computer files while repeatedly glancing up at my face to see if I'm a match for whichever mug shot they have on the screen. All the while, my mind is flashing back nervously to every indiscretion I've ever had in my life and wondering if the jig was up.

Could they be after me for a dumpling I swiped off of my colleague's all you can eat tray when I had only ordered a bowl of noodles? Did the hotel clerk snitch on me for taking one too many toiletries? Is it possible that they saw me buy that "Rolex" off a street vender in Hong Kong that was on sale for seven dollars?

China, despite all the economic reforms they've had over the last 20 years, is still after all, a communist country. I have an irrational fear that if I don't answer all their questions correctly, I'll immediately be whisked off to some Mongolian labor camp.

My colleague, who is always with me when we cross the border (and seems amused by the whole situation), once observed that the longer a customs agent questions me, the more my voice changes.

At first, I start out speaking Chinese. Once their questions get more pointed, I immediately revert to English. Any further questions and my American accent becomes more pronounced. The more inquisitive they get, the more I sound like I was born and raised in California. For some irrational reason, on a subconscious level I've concluded that they will assume Californians are never wanton criminals. I start using the words "dude" and "righteous" in my responses as much as possible.

By the end of the screening, I've become a professional surfer, spouting phrases like, "Dude! I'm like toootally here for a righteous business convention dude!"

Do they really think a dangerous criminal would try to get through customs sounding like that while wearing running shorts and a Daffy Duck T-shirt?

Of course, this latest trip added another component to the customs process – the SARS inspection.

While the SARS outbreak was apparently completely under control by the time of my visit, government officials were still very diligent in monitoring each person as they passed the customs counter, ready to detain anyone with any telltale symptoms. I became acutely aware of my desire to contain any impulse I might have to sneeze at that particular moment.

If I did, I suppose I could say, "My bad, dude. I like toootally have a case of the hay fever, dude."

Learning the ABC's of Chinese - Minus the ABC's

I am in the midst of an identity crisis – or maybe it's a panic attack. Even worse, maybe it's both.

Last week I took my six-year-old son to Chinese School. For those who may have read some of my earlier columns, you should already know about my Chinese language competency. For those of you that haven't, let me describe it this way: My Chinese is like a soufflé – it starts out big and beautiful, but once you dig into it you find that there's not much substance and filled with hot air.

People have told me that the intonation and phrasing of my Chinese is very good. The problem is that my vocabulary would put a four year old to shame.

I am the first to admit my limitations when it comes to the Chinese language, which is one of the reasons why we decided to send my son to Chinese school so that he could get a head start. But I'm not about to admit my weaknesses to my own son.

When my wife signed him up for the class, I made it perfectly clear what my responsibilities would be – I would take him to and from class. I would sit with him during class to make sure he paid attention. But I made it perfectly clear – I was not about to teach him myself or be a teacher's aid. We had an agreement. We had a pact.

I knew there was a problem the minute we sat down to class. The teacher immediately started directing the parents on what she wanted us to do to help while we were in session. Every word the teacher said was in Chinese. Every utterance. Even what she wrote on the chalkboard…all Chinese. I'm sure people could tell that we were father and son by the same distant expression we had on our faces.

Oh sure, I understood a few things. She started out by introducing herself, told us she was excited to be here, and then asked us to open our workbooks. After that, yada, yada, yada. She could have been telling us to run for our lives to escape a marauding pack of killer cocker spaniels, but you'd never know it by the way that I was frantically flipping through the work book trying to get some inkling as to what she was talking about.

What is a father to do when his six-year-old son asks him, "Daddy, what is she saying? What does she want me to do?" As I was as clueless as he, the only thing I could come up with was, "Look, if you're not going to pay attention, I'm certainly not going to tell you!"

They say that in order to overcome a traumatic experience, the average person must go through the five stages of resolution: (1) denial, (2) bargaining, (3) anger, (4) despair, and (5) acceptance. You could certainly see me going through each of these stages whenever I responded to the teacher's questions.

Denial – "Yes, I'd be happy to answer that question, but my ears are still ringing after going to a heavy metal concert last night and I can't hear you. It was so totally rad."

Bargaining – "I'd be happy to answer that question if you'd first answer my question: Why is there air?"

Anger – "Why are you asking me this question?!? I'm only the driver! Please call my wife. We had a pact."

Despair – "I'm sorry. I can't answer your question. It brings up painful memories from my childhood."

Acceptance – "Excuse me? This is Chinese class? I'm sorry, wrong class. C'mon son, let's go."

Hmm…that last one seems like I skipped over *acceptance* and went back around to *denial*. Well, four out of five's not bad.

The Kitchen God and His Missing Dumplings

Nian! It's all his fault.

For those of you who aren't familiar with him, *Nian* is a monster and legend has it that on the eve of Chinese New Year, *Nian* materializes and devours unsuspecting families.

I know now that the custom of setting off firecrackers, lighting lanterns and hanging red couplets was designed to scare off *Nian*, who hates loud noises, fire, and the color red. As a youngster, all of this was just an excuse for me to play with firecrackers.

I'm sure my parents did share some of the customs. But when you're an impressionable boy, it's hard to separate fact from fiction.

Case in point: The mystery of the missing dumplings.

One custom practiced during Chinese New Year is to set aside an offering of food for the Kitchen God who visits every year to provide spiritual comfort. I remember watching each year as my Aunt Lucy would set aside a plate of dumplings and other goodies at night on a table near the fireplace.

The strange thing was, several dumplings would always be missing in the morning. *Actual* dumplings were gone, which even as a nine year old I realized was abnormal, for even the milk and cookies I put out on Christmas Eve for Santa Claus were always still there when I woke up in the morning. The Kitchen God eats the dumpling in a spiritual sense, not a real one.

I decided to investigate and see who was swiping the dumplings from under the Kitchen God's nose. That night, with everyone asleep, I crept out of bed and crawled ever so quietly down the hallway so that I could catch the malcontent in the act. At the end of the hall, I peered around the corner to the fireplace to wait. And wait. And wait.

Then, in a flash, I identified the culprit, and I was devastated. Who would have thought?

Nian had overcome and inhabited the body of *Bubbles*, our Cocker Spaniel. I should have suspected it earlier that evening when I saw the dog run off every time I lit off a firecracker.

Crouching Child, Bedeviled Parent

I had a grueling day yesterday. I wasn't sure if I was going to make it, but I did. Mentally, I was completely drained. Physically, I was a wreck.

What one word best describes the experience? Well, let's see.

According to Webster's New World Dictionary, the following is the definition for the word, "burnout".

Burnout (pronounced, "bern'out'"): A state of emotional exhaustion caused by the stresses of one's work or responsibilities.

A state of emotional exhaustion. Umm, yes, that would be me. That's not quite concise enough, though. I've come up with the perfect phrase to sum up how I feel as well as identify what I went through yesterday.

Disneyland Burnout (pronounced, "Augghh!!!"): A state of emotional exhaustion caused by interminably long lines, exorbitantly priced food, and the inexplicable and sudden appearance of clothes wearing, human-sized rodents.

Now don't get me wrong. This is the same Disneyland I grew up cherishing as a kid. It's the same Disneyland I would have gladly traded my younger brother for to get a chance to ride on the latest ride. And it's the same Disneyland that I would beg my parents to take me to year after year after year.

Unfortunately, therein lies the problem. It's one thing when you are the beggar. It's a whole other thing when you are the begg-ee.

For those of you who think I'm exaggerating, let me give you an idea of how our little family outing went.

Let's start with the afore-mentioned pleading. My eight-year-old son Tyler, who is usually a bright, unassuming delight to be with, was great fun to be with when we were actually on one of the rides itself. Unfortunately, each ride usually lasts for about three minutes, which is then followed by about 40 minutes of us waiting in line for to go on another three-minute ride. It's during each of these little interludes that we were subjected to my son's version of "closing the deal."

His sales pitch usually goes something like this:

Can we go on Space Mountain one more time? Please? I always love going on Space Mountain. Oh please! PLEASE??? JUST…PLEASE?!? I just want to go on Space Mountain one more time! PLEASE? PLEAASE??? PLEAAAAASE???

Bear in mind that it's during the second round of this that he's clasping his hands in a tight grip, shaking his hands urgently with his eyes closed and slightly bent at the knees.

Apparently, he seems to believe that this elevated level of groveling has a chance at succeeding. Anyone watching this scene from a distance might think that this was a starving boy begging for sustenance.

Speaking of food, being thrown side to side on some of the faster rides can leave you hungry, tired, and thirsty. No problem there, because we can take a quick break and as a convenience, food and refreshments are all around. A nice, cold, bottled water and some tasty french fries would hit the spot.

How much? Eleven dollars.

Eleven dollars? Eleven dollars for some water and half a potato? Ah well, at least the french fries weren't in the shape of Mickey Mouse.

For some reason, anything in the park that even remotely resembles a circle, like a balloon, waffles, and especially hats, must be re-designed to include two round ears protruding from the top of it. I think it's mandated in one of Disney's bylaws.

Why, even the week before, as I was in Asia traveling from the Hong Kong airport into the city via their express train, I saw, out the window, another train with a big Mickey Mouse emblem stamped on it's side. This reminded me that, of course, this was the train to take some happy tourists to Disney's newest Disneyworld, this one located in Hong Kong.

And if you looked closely enough at the train, you could see some parents, many of them wearing "Mickey" hats, seated on the train. Right below them, no doubt, would be their kids, hands clasped, in the Disney "crouch position."

Dressed to the Nines – or Maybe Just Four and a Half

They say that men are from Mars, and women are from Venus. I don't know much about that, but what I do know is that wherever the men are, they are dressed in comfortable clothes.

My wife Maya and I are having a disagreement over some of my clothes. Specifically, some of the old t-shirts I wear around the house. For some mysterious reason, she'd like to donate a number of these shirts to Goodwill because they are, in her words, "too worn out and disgusting to wear anymore".

Then she makes the smart-alecky comment that she probably can't donate them because "Goodwill probably wouldn't take them."

Let me just set the record straight. I own some nice clothes. Whenever I need to attend a business meeting, a wedding, or other formal occasion, I'm prepared.

But, the fact of the matter is, I work at home. I spend most of my day writing e-mails and making phone calls. I just don't see the point of wearing nicer clothes at home when there's nobody there (except the family) to see it. My wearing nicer clothes probably won't impress them and certainly won't impress me.

Still, Maya seems pretty adamant about the whole thing. She's repeatedly mentioned, half-jokingly I hope, that at some point while I'm out of the house, several of these shirts will suddenly disappear, and I will be forced to break in a whole new set of clothes.

Not wanting to let this matter go without a fight, I decided to take a stand with the handful of shirts in question to hopefully delay their demise for a bit longer. So last night, I sat down to write a little note, which I subsequently pinned to one of the shirts she finds most disagreeable, and put it on her vanity to discover.

This is what I wrote:

Dear Maya,

I am soliciting your input in regards to the attached article of clothing.

It has come to my attention that you have some objections at my continued wearing of said garment.

I would greatly appreciate any input you may have that might help me determine what to do with the shirt mentioned above.

Apparently, you feel that this shirt is too worn out with holes and stains for me to continue wearing. However, it is my belief that this shirt still retains some intrinsic value.

Every frayed seam represents a unique moment of my life. The oil spot on the left side of the shirt brings back fond memories of a terrific dim sum meal. The hole near the collar brings me back to a classic Sunday afternoon touch football game where I scored the winning touchdown.

I've worn this shirt with pride, and through the years this shirt has earned my respect for what it and I have gone through together. It is quite literally – a part of the fabric of my life.

This is why, at this point, I am leaning towards keeping the shirt for several more years.

As I said, any input you can provide will be greatly appreciated, unless your opinion is that I get rid of the shirt, in which case, I should let you know that I keep an inventory of these shirts, and it will immediately become apparent if one or more of them suddenly makes an unexpected departure.

Your loving (and comfortable) husband,
Wayne

A Duck for the Ages

What is that old saying? *Absence makes the heart grow fonder?*

It's a common saying that usually pertains to how you feel when a person you care about is gone for an extended period of time. The longer they are away, the more you look forward to them coming home again.

I've discovered that this rule applies to any number of things that might be missing in your life. For example, I'm growing more and more fond of pizza by the minute.

My ever-growing fondness for pizza notwithstanding, I think the perfect example of this axiom has to do with my dad.

Ever since I can remember, from the time that I was a little boy, I can remember times when Dad would reminisce about his past. My dad did not have a very good memory, so when he did remember something, especially if it was something good, it tended to stand out.

So what would be the one pleasant memory my dad would consistently bring up? Coming to America to start a new life? No. Getting married and watching the love of his life walk down the aisle? No. The birth of his children? No.

He talked about the one time my mom made a roasted duck for dinner.

She made this duck before I was born and this was no ordinary duck dish. This was a duck made with taro, and according to Dad, it was dee-licious.

You have to remember – the duck in question was roasted in the early sixties. This duck was hatched during the Kennedy administration. There have been fourteen Olympic games held since that duck was served. I was born shortly after the duck and while I'm sure he was very happy holding his first born son for the first time, I imagine he was thinking how much better the day would be if there was another roasted duck waiting for them on the way home from the hospital.

But it was not to be. In fact, my mom never made that duck dish again.

Oh sure, she's roasted plenty of ducks since then. She made ducks during the Johnson administration, through Watergate, and during the cold war. But not that particular duck recipe.

There was no taro in all the subsequent ducks.

I know how my dad felt. Along with the celebrated duck, my mom once made sweet and sour pork. Now, we all know how easy it is to find sweet and sour pork. Every Chinese restaurant makes it every single day. But my mom made it once and only once. No repeat performances. I can understand someone trying out a recipe and never making it again if it turned out badly. But in the case of dad's duck and my pork, it turned out great. It was good. *Very* good. It was drool worthy.

On the other hand, Mom attempts to make a Thanksgiving turkey every year and every year it comes out so dry it's closer to beef jerky than a roast turkey. It's so dry that any gravy in the vicinity of the turkey turns to powder once the turkey sucks all the moisture out of it. *This* we get every year.

I'm not sure I understand the logic of it. I suppose if there were some way we could change the constitution so that ducks and sweet and sour pork replaced turkey and gravy during Thanksgiving, we'd be all set.

The problem is, it had been so long since Dad enjoyed that single, solitary duck, that his enjoyment of said duck had grown to mythic proportions. The way he talked about that duck, you'd think this duck was manna from the heavens.

I don't think any chef, much less my mom, could roast a duck in a way that could match the expectations my dad had created. A duck that is served only once every forty years?

I'm afraid dad would have passed out from the anticipation. It might even coin a new saying.

Absence makes the heart have irregular palpitations.

Eight Words of Wisdom

Maybe we should go to China this year.

Eight words that immediately bring a shiver to my spine. Eight words that I have been dreading for the past two years.

These are the eight words my wife Maya used yesterday to officially announce that we will begin planning a family trip to China some time this year.

Our children are now eleven, and given that we are an Asian American family, apparently once they have reached their pre-teen years, we have a fiduciary responsibility to introduce our spawn to their "roots".

I know there are those of you out there who are thinking, "This is an adventure, Wayne! Enjoy the experience of watching your kids discover their heritage. They'll get to climb the Great Wall! They'll stroll down the Bund in Shanghai. They'll get to see a part of recent history by visiting the Bird's Nest from last year's Olympics! Stop complaining and treasure this!!!"

Fair enough. All of that is true. But you've left out a few things.

Let's start with when we'll actually be going to China. Given the kid's school schedule and when we can logically take an extended vacation, the only time we'll be able to go is in the summer. Summer in China – a month long sauna. We'll be walking in heat that is so oppressive it's only suited for lizards and Kenyan marathon runners. And since I'm the only one strong enough in the family to carry my wife's oversized luggage, I'll be the only Kenyan marathon runner carrying around a 50-pound backpack.

Of course, in most of the main cities in China – Beijing, Shanghai, and Hong Kong, all the newer hotels have air conditioning. And, perhaps as a way of compensating for the oppressive heat in the summer, most hotels blast their air conditioners so low that when I walk in from outside, I'll be the only Kenyan marathon runner carrying around a 50 pound backpack wearing shorts, a t-shirt and a winter ski jacket.

Then there are the children. Ah yes, our three impressionable children.

Having gone to China repeatedly over the last fifteen years for business, I know that the flight is around 14 hours. If I recall, the last time we had a family trip and took a one-hour flight to Las Vegas, I had to answer the question, "Are we there yet?" 27 times.

Once we arrive in China, most likely in Hong Kong first, our kids will undoubtedly discover that lo and behold, there is a Disneyworld in Hong Kong! For at least a day, I will likely discover the joy in my kid's eyes, as they make their way through the Magic Kingdom, in order to ride on the same rides they have ridden on a hundred times at the Disneyland that is only a couple hours away from home, and listen to "It's a small world" in Chinese while enduring heat that is suitable only for a lizard or a Kenyan marathon runner carrying a 50 pound backpack and wearing Mickey Mouse hat.

OK, OK, enough with the cynicism. I'm just kidding…well, half kidding anyways. The truth is, I think I'll actually get a kick out of taking my kids to China for the first time. For the first time, they'll walk down the street and not feel like they're the odd man out. For the first time, they'll know what it's like to live in a place where the people around them look like them.

When I was in my teens, I felt that experience. I went to China on my own. It was a life changing experience. I went to China with the expectation that it would be an overseas "Spring Break", but I came back profoundly changed. I looked at the world differently.

I met people who were integral to my parent's lives, and by extension, my own. I learned that the Mandarin dialect I had reluctantly used only with my parents, was actually a gift that connected me to generations of family before me.

If not for that one trip, I doubt that I would have married the love of my life, who was born and raised in Taiwan. So in all seriousness, "Maybe we **should** go to China this year."

I went to China that year as an American who happened to be Asian. I came back as an Asian American.

Eliminating the Gray Area

It's amazing where life's lessons can unexpectedly come from. In this case, my nine-year-old son taught me a lesson on the dangers of vanity.

Anyone who knows me will tell you that I'm not a vain person. In fact, anyone who saw me walk into the International House of Pancakes last weekend wearing my standard issue tattered sweater, oversized sweatpants, and four day old stubble will back me up on that one.

The only exception to my own lack of vanity comes with the pride I have in my hair. No, I'm not talking about spending a lot of money sporting the latest hairstyle (I believe you'd call my latest style "Roll out of bed crapshoot"), or combing in a sleek hair gel.

The source of my pride comes from the fact that unlike myself, the hair on most of my friends (and even my younger brother) are well on their way to turning gray if not falling out altogether. I, on the other hand, continue to have a full head of hair, still as dark as when I was a kid.

I don't know why my lack of gray is so important to me. Maybe it's a way of clinging to my youth. Maybe the contrast of my hair compared to my friends allows me the enjoyment of saying, "Hey, you're an old man!" without actually having to say anything.

The problem with this kind of vanity, of course, is that it is fleeting. Time inexorably marches on, and sooner or later you have to face reality (or a good hair dye).

It doesn't happen all of a sudden. It creeps up on you. The first gray hair I saw in the mirror a few months ago, I easily dismissed as a "genetic anomaly". It's a one-off. An imperfection in a sea of black, youthful goodness. Besides, I kept thinking, it's just one gray hair.

Then a few weeks go by, and alongside that one gray hair sprouts up a few new gray haired residents in what was before a perfectly youthful head of hair. The truth is that these new sprouts of grey were virtually unnoticeable by any uninformed passersby, but due to my already established vanity and the fact that I've painstakingly categorized each follicle of hair, each withered strand was an assault on my already fragile ego.

Staring at the mirror, observing the gradual and inevitable mark of time, you discover an opportunity, a crossroads in your life where you can set aside petty notions of vanity, and truly value the life you have with all your lifelong friends and loved ones. You can spend your days accepting the wisdom that comes with getting older, and realizing that the color of your hair is meaningless in the greater scheme of life.

Or, you can do what I did and frantically start pulling out those noxious strands of gray hair.

Which leads me to my hard earned lesson.

You quickly realize that staring at the mirror only allows you to pull out a few conveniently placed strands of hair growing towards the front of your head. After that, the hairs toward the back of your head are nearly impossible to pluck by yourself. A second mirror, a magnifying glass, tweezers, a complex series of ropes and pulleys…at some point you realize that you can't pull them all out on your own.

Just as I'm about to give up, my son Tyler walks over and asks for some help on his homework. As a responsible father, understanding completely the importance of homework, I tell Tyler to put his books down and help me pull out the remaining gray hairs so that we can quickly get to his homework.

Tyler, always the helpful one, is exceedingly eager to help me out. He stands behind me as I'm seated, and peers into the back of my head, literally digging through my hair, trying to identify each lonely strand of gray hair.

He doesn't want to hurt me, and thinks that by pulling each hair out slowly it will hurt less. I quickly correct him after the first pull by threatening to withhold his allowance for the rest of the year if he pulled another hair out slowly.

He quickly gets the hang of things. A quick pluck here, a short yank there.

He's pulled out four or five gray hairs in a matter of seconds. At one point, Tyler says, "Hey, I'm your own personal monkey!"

So we come to the last gray hair, and it's right on the back of my head, and it's too short for Tyler to get a good hold of it. So, he suggests, that he guide my hand to the back of my head, help me grasp that single strand, and let my stronger hands do the trick.

Once it's ready, Tyler tells me to pull. He says, "Now, Dad!" I yank.

It was like getting your hair caught in the trunk of someone's car as they were speeding away. I had pulled out about 20 hairs, and as it turns out, not one of them was gray.

My son had inadvertently gotten me to voluntarily yank a big clump of hair out of my own head.

Tomorrow I'm spending his allowance on hair dye.

A Time for Reflection, Resolutions, and Calcium Supplements

And so, as we reach the zenith of another year, we pause to reflect on the year that was, of lessons learned, and the promise of a new year. Such as it is with the close of another year, I come to the realization that in my life, time begets wisdom, experience begets patience, and perhaps most importantly, I am one step closer to needing soluble fiber supplements in my daily diet. I wonder where I can get a bulk discount on Metamucil?

If at all else, I've learned that time creeps up on you. For example, a few weeks ago, I hurt my leg and was walking with a noticeable limp. This, in and of it self was not remarkable. Rarely does a year in my life go by that I don't cause significant injury to myself by doing something needlessly dangerous. Try to fly off the roof with homemade "Bat-wings?" Check. Run and jump off a trampoline to dunk a basketball like Michael Jordan? Check. Try to leap over a four-foot hedge to impress my wife? Check.

No, what set this injury apart from all the rest was that it occurred while I was walking around, looking around. I didn't trip. I didn't walk into a potted azalea. I caused significant injury to my leg from the simple act of walking.

I believe that life has a purpose. Every aspect of life is an opportunity to grow and learn. Still, what practical purpose would an "age-inflicted" injury serve my life and those around me? It took a while for me to discover the answer, and the meaning was revealed the moment someone asked me how I injured my leg.

It dawned on me that the answer I would give to that seemingly innocuous question would reveal the level of maturity I've attained over my life. Would I own up to the fact that I had caused myself a nearly debilitating injury from the simple act of walking from my front door to the mailbox a half block away? Or would I revel in my own state of denial by coming up with a more impressive and non-age related explanation?

In the end, I provided my questioner a very logical and reasonable explanation for my injury. If I recall, the explanation included the presence of an oak tree, a beehive, a ladder and a rottweiler.

My own issues of denial notwithstanding, I did learn some things this year.

For several months now, my seven-year-old son has been writing ever more persuasive letters to Santa, beseeching him to get him an electronic toy called a "Roboraptor." This robot, which is basically a roboticized dinosaur that moves and makes monster sounds via a remote control, costs $120.00.

I mention the price of this toy primarily as a point of reference, for if I recall correctly, it was only a few years ago that this same son, when he was three years old, would have been perfectly happy if I had given him a box of bubble wrap for Christmas.

Still, my son isn't normally a very materialistic person, and the years of bubble wrap for presents certainly served their purpose. Besides, he had indeed earned a present with his grades and good behavior at school. So, I figured, I'd splurge a little and Santa would have to lug around an extra "Roboraptor" for this year's deliveries.

Christmas morning. Excitement was in the air. You could almost see "Roboraptor" straining against his box to escape and fulfill a boy's wildest dreams.

When it came to his turn to open his presents, my son ripped open the package, and he immediately squealed with a shriek of delight. "Roboraptor" was at last his, and he proceeded to act out all his prehistoric fantasies with his new robo pal in tow.

He played ecstatically with his new toy with joyous abandon and rapturous attention…for about 20 minutes. He promptly spent the next half hour popping the bubble wrap that was packed around the "Roboraptor" box.

By my calculations, each minute my son played with "Roboraptor" cost me about six dollars. As always, the bubble wrap was free.

Next year, he says, he wants a lava lamp. I wonder what type of packing material they use for that?

English is Perfect — Know What I mean?

Quick! Someone define the word, "Contradiction". Let me take a stab.

"Contradiction. Central-American rebels who enunciate perfectly. Contra-diction."

Ok, maybe not.

The word "contradiction" is a perfect example of the idiosyncrasies of the English language. In other words, the word "contradiction" is in itself a contradiction.

My wife Maya was born and raised in Taiwan, and came to the U.S. for college and has stayed here ever since. She learned to speak perfect English, which absolutely amazes me. It amazes me that anyone whose first language wasn't English can figure out this confounding language that seems to have so many contradictions. She can even speak English while simultaneously tapping her head and rubbing her tummy.

In many respects, English is a language where just about anything goes. In the end, communicating in English has less to do with what you actually said and more to do with what you really mean. It's a very "loosey-goosey" language. Why that phrase refers to a very limber bird is beyond me, but *you know what I mean*.

Here are some perfect examples of English that don't make obvious sense:

1. *Breakfast* is what you eat in the morning. It's not a time to take a *break* from eating to go on a *fast*.
2. You can *draw* a picture, but you can also *draw* a bath, *draw* a breath, *draw* someone's attention or *draw* a conclusion. Is there anything you can't draw?
3. Creature comforts are for people.
4. A formula is a mathematical equation as well as something you feed a baby.

Even for those of us who speak English, there are two types of English. One English for the general population, and another English specifically for professional athletes. You can refer to this form of English as "Jock-ish".

Watch any sports channel on TV while a professional athlete is being interviewed – you almost need subtitles to know what they are talking about.

Ask your average "Joe Athlete" a question like, "Hey Joe, how do you feel?" after a big game and you will most likely hear a response like:

I gave 120% to that game. Could I have done better? Yes. Did I prepare enough for the game? Yes. Would I have done anything different? No. When you have a Joe Athlete go on the field, you have to play like you know you're going to win. A Joe Athlete will always put in 150% to help his team win. Would I have liked to win? Yes. Will we ever get another chance? I hope so.

Are you asking and answering your own questions? Yes. Are you referring to yourself in the 3rd person? Yes. Would putting in 150% of effort risk violating the time and space continuum? Possibly.

One of these days, I'm going to walk into a Denny's restaurant and order my breakfast like a professional athlete.

"Yes, I'm ready to order. Do I want pancakes? Yes. Would a half-stack be enough? No. Would I like my eggs scrambled? Yes. A Wayne Chan never likes his eggs runny. Would I like two or four links of sausage? Two. Does it look like you've stopped taking my order to call for security? Yes. Do I need to give it 170% to finish all my food before security arrives? Yes.

It probably wouldn't help for me to tap my head and rub my tummy while I'm eating either.

Not a Cloud in the Sky
– on Purpose

I read recently that in preparation for the 2008 Summer Olympics, the host country of China has been testing technology that would allow them to control the atmosphere to ensure that the games will be held in picture perfect weather.

That being the case, for the first time in Olympic history, when the athletes take the field, notice the crisp blue skies overhead and proclaim, "You couldn't ask for better weather", an official can rightly say, "Well, actually you can, but it takes a while to get the permits."

As I understand it, the technology has been around for years, and it involves shooting certain chemicals into clouds that are heading towards the Olympics to force the clouds to rain and sputter out by the time they pass over Beijing, where the games are being held.

Think about it – we now have the power to CHANGE THE WEATHER! If we keep going in this direction, you just know that at some point the Sharper Image is going to come out with a personal "Thunderstorm Zapper" for those days when you "really can't afford to let it rain."

Umbrella companies will go belly up. No need to take any more chances when washing your car and hoping that it doesn't start raining the next day. No more hurricanes to deal with and if one happens to slip through, you can send a nasty letter to the National Weather Service to fire the guy who apparently fell asleep at the wheel (or in this case, fell asleep at the big weather canon).

You have to wonder about the guy who came up with this technology and the type of personality he had. If I was in that meeting when he proposed the idea, I know what I'd ask.

Me: Excuse me, but do you really think it's a good idea to tamper with Mother Nature and do we really know what the long term consequences might be?

Weather Changing Inventor Guy: Mother Nature sucks. Besides, I can make it rain!

Of course, if you ask an environmentalist like former Vice President Al Gore, he might say that we've had the power to change the weather for quite a while but until recently, we just didn't know it. Who would have ever thought that as a collective force, we human beings would have the power to make our world warmer?

On the one hand the idea of mankind having the audacity to control the weather is kind of funny. But when you really think about it, it seems like it's a part of a much larger trend, one that at least for me, seems a little scary.

We've built enormous dams to generate electricity and divert water to where it wasn't meant to go. As we saw with hurricane Katrina, we've built entire cities in areas that lie ten feet below sea level and are shocked when a massive storm fills it to the rim with water.

Now we are planning to physically prevent the possibility of rain on the opening day of a very famous sporting event, as athletes from all over the world march onto the field in front of an adoring crowd.

Call me crazy, but maybe just this once, it wouldn't necessarily be the worst thing for it to rain on this parade.

A Bouncing Ball and a Bruised Ego

There comes a time when you look back on your life and recall the moments when you truly accomplished something special. For some, it might be a physical act, like climbing Mt. Everest or finishing a marathon. For others, it could be a creative act, like writing a best selling novel, or inventing a better mousetrap.

When I look back, I am proud of being a good father and husband. But, the more I contemplate my accomplishments, the more I keep going back to the one success that towers over the rest.

I finally beat my mother in law in a game of ping pong.

Immature, you say? Insignificant, you proclaim? Let me explain.

My mother in law was born and raised in Taiwan. Every day during lunch, as well as three nights a week, she gets together with friends to play ping pong. She is consistently the league champion.

As for me, I get as competitive as you can possibly imagine. I will risk serious bodily injury and humiliation in order to win a point.

When she arrived in San Diego, my first instinct was to play nice. After all, I was the future son-in-law, and the reason that her daughter was moving from Taiwan for good. Fairly early on, she suggested we play ping pong. Sounded innocent enough, and while I don't play that much, I figured heck, I'll even let her win.

The first match set the tone. Not only was she beating me, she was blowing me away, and to make things worse, I could tell that she was taunting me in Chinese as well.

"I'm sure you can beat me", she said.
"Should I hit it softer?"

For the next few days, I knew my mission in life. No need for sleep or food. I became one with the ping pong paddle.

We played over 30 matches. I never won, but at least I heard some new taunts.

"Maybe you should try playing left handed...or maybe I should."
"Where are my glasses? I can't believe I'm winning without my glasses."

The next day, she was gone, back to Taiwan. My official ping pong record was zero wins, 35 losses. With each day that passed, I muddled through with no purpose in life. A broken shell of a man.

Fortunately for me, a few months passed and she called to say she would be visiting us again. The clouds lifted. Time for a rematch.

She arrived, and after exchanging pleasantries, we got down to business. The first ten games were a replay of the last trip.

But then came the 11th game. I could do no wrong. I have never played so well, before or since. Final score: 21-18. Game over. My new record: one win, 45 losses.

She wanted to keep playing, but there would be no rematch. I would finish my career with a win.

Does it make any difference that she had jet lag from her 12 hour flight here, or that I'm twice her size, 20 years younger or that she still has a 44 game advantage over me?

Nah. A win is a win in my book.

Not the Best or Worst of Times – But Somewhere in the Middle

Everything in moderation.

The basic idea is that life has its ups and downs and the best way to make your way through it is to avoid extremes on either end. When all is said and done, you'll find that besides winning the lottery and falling off a cliff, most of your life will be spent somewhere in the middle.

In much of Asia, it's called, "The Middle Way", and it's a rule of thought that is prevalent throughout Asian culture. Don't get too exuberant or too distraught. Keep perspective on things. If many Asians seem to be reserved in their demeanor, I would venture to say it's because of "the middle way."

It's a concept that seems to have lost favor here in the West. Our lives are filled with extremes. Just look at the movies.

When was the last time you saw a "good" movie? If you go by the one or two line reviews in the movie section of your local newspaper, none of us have seen a "good" movie in years.

Oh, I've seen movies recently that I've really enjoyed. But it wasn't "good". According to the reviewer, it was a "Swashbuckling film, bristling with excitement and one of the finest cinematic adventures in years."

I see. I must have missed something. I just thought it was a funny movie.

Then there's the "Two Thumbs Up!" rating that reviewers Roger Ebert and Richard Roeper give to movies they recommend. From my understanding, there's no amount of publicity a studio can buy that is worth more than getting a "Two Thumbs Up!" rating from Ebert and Roeper.

The problem is, nearly every movie in the movie section has a "Two Thumbs Up!" rating by Ebert and Roeper. How is that going to help me decide which movie to watch?

The other day, I saw that one movie ad with a rating from Ebert and Roeper using the words, "Two Thumbs Up! Way, WAY UP!"

What does that mean? What am I supposed to do with that?

Apparently, the fact that their thumbs are up is no longer enough to help me in my movie watching decision. Now, I need to pay attention to the elevation of their thumbs in the air.

So, the question I have is, how would they rate a truly once in a lifetime, groundbreaking film? I mean, they'd have to write something like, "Two Thumbs Up! Way, WAY UP! We are standing on chairs with our thumbs up high! If we could surgically remove our thumbs, we'd be shooting them in the air – that's how UP we are! Look! We are waving our feet in the air! Our thumbs as well as our toes are UP!!!"

On the other hand, the other end of the spectrum isn't safe from our excesses either.

Last week I was watching a sports program devoted to the latest controversy around athlete and the use of steroids in baseball. According to the experts, the prevalent use of steroids has become a "tragedy of mythic proportions" for baseball.

I don't know the exact criteria you would use to determine a tragedy. But in the greater scheme of things, I'm not sure taking an illegal drug to help a player hit a white ball out of a stadium could technically be considered a tragedy of mythic proportions.

I'm not saying I'd give it "two thumbs up", mind you. I'd give it a definite "Thumbs down." In this case, two very muscular "thumbs down."

A Picture Perfect Picture
A Pain to Perfect

Author's Note: *Out of our personal privacy, I wrote the following column without addressing the fact that two of our kids (out of triplets) are on the autism spectrum. A few years later, I decided to address it in the column following this one.*

Ahh…the annual family photo.

The kid's birthday is coming up and to celebrate that auspicious occasion, we reserve an afternoon to take a family photo to serve as a marker of another year gone by. Just this once, maybe it won't make my wife and I a nervous wreck.

It's not that I don't like our annual family photos. Actually, I cherish each and every one of them. Each one is a testament to another year of growth and discovery for our three kids.

It's taking the picture that's torture.

You see, my wife Maya and I are the proud parents of nine year old triplets, which, of course, means that I spend the bulk of my time each day either at parent/teacher meetings or buying a squadron's worth of rations at Costco.

Anyways, our picture-taking day always starts out with the location. Which picturesque setting would be the perfect background to display our happy, well adjusted family? Maybe this year we'll find the perfect spot with the skyline of San Diego behind us, or perhaps on a sandy beach in La Jolla. There's no shortage of scenic locales here in San Diego. Finding a location is a snap.

This however, will be the last sane and simple decision we will make for the rest of the day.

We drive out to the location. We walk out to the picture perfect spot, I set up a few chairs or a blanket to sit on, as well as the camera and a tripod.

Maya and I sit down, we have the kids sit around us, we wait until sunset to get the perfect lighting we want, and we ask our babysitter to start taking pictures. She tries to get the kid's attention to look at the camera and snap the picture.

As with every other year, the babysitter will fail. It's not the babysitter's fault, mind you. For whatever reason, if you set up a camera in front of us in an idyllic setting, the one place our kids will not look is at the camera.

Of course, maybe I'm just being too demanding. If I was just going for a picture of my kids looking at their shoelaces, or having one of them flick the other's ears, or maybe have one of them kick me in the shin, no problem – mission accomplished.

No, being the particular person that I am, I'd like them to smile for the camera for the picture perfect shot. Which means, I have to start yelling.

Ethan, look at the camera!
Savannah, look at the camera!
Ethan & Savannah, look at the camera!
Tyler, stop looking at me. Look at the camera!
We'll go when I say we can go!
Put that down!
Take that grass out of your mouth!
Good Ethan! Now smile!
No! Smile and look at the camera!
Come back here!
Put your hands down!
Who's kicking me?!?
Stop kicking and look at the camera!

And of course, there's always the popular, "Look happy or so help me…"

Of the 170 plus shots that were taken, 87% of the photos have one or more of the children not looking at the camera, 10% have one or more of the children not in the picture for various juvenile reasons, and the remaining 3% are unusable because either Maya or myself are glaring at the children, most likely in the middle of browbeating our kids to look at the camera.

If you haven't already noticed, that means that with all that effort, as with every other year we've tried this, we didn't get a single solitary picture we could use.

Fortunately, we live in the age of digital cameras and photo-editing software, which means that a picture perfect family photo is just a few clicks of the mouse away.

Some purists may say that digitally lopping off heads from one picture and pasting them into others makes the finished photo a fabrication or a farce. For the most part, I agree with them. At least I have my limits.

I'm willing to digitally clip out a happy smiling face from each of the kids in various snapshots and cobble them all together for the perfect photographic illusion. I'm perfectly happy to adjust the brightness or contrast of the picture if that improves the picture. But when my wife looks at the picture as I'm manipulating it on the computer screen and asks me to "fix her hair", that's when I draw the line.

Once you go down that slippery slope, there's no limit to the "improvements" you can make. I might decide to drop a few pounds, or maybe I can "upgrade" the steel watch I'm wearing to a gold Rolex. Maybe the beach background would look better with some perfectly placed coconut trees with a sign hanging from it that reads "Welcome to Waikiki."

For the past nine years, we've managed to create, what I call, a "realistic illusion." In the end, our annual family photo is never completely real, but that's really beside the point.

I love these perfect pictures not for the picture itself, but for what it represents. It shows a perfectly happy family together, and there's nothing fake about that.

A Picture is Worth a Thousand Edits

I was beginning to lose my breath. Standing behind the tripod, centering my family in the camera's viewfinder, and running back into the picture before the timer ran down to snap a picture ought to be easy enough. It becomes more of a challenge when the subjects of your picture include your six-year-old triplets, who have no intention to sit still, smile, and look into the camera for a family portrait. Add to the fact that two of our triplets are autistic, and it's no wonder why we were on our 27th take.

It might as well have been our 270th take. The very nature of autism, a developmental disorder that begins in early childhood and robs those afflicted with the ability to socially interact with those around them, makes it difficult for them to maintain eye contact with others, much less a camera lens.

Of course, I never expected that I would manage to snap the perfect Polaroid moment. As with years past, my goal was to snap enough pictures to individually catch each of the children smiling at the camera so that I could digitally cut and paste their faces together and artificially create the perfect family picture. I know the final picture isn't going to be completely authentic, but at least I managed to draw a line in the sand when I objected to my wife's request to "fix" her hair.

After so long of struggling and then adjusting to our children's condition, you wonder why anyone would go to such great lengths to create this minor illusion. Having one more seemingly traditional family photo hanging on the wall certainly wouldn't let us forget the reality of our lives. Sending the photo out to friends and family only serves to remind them how *normal* our children *can* look.

Perhaps the picture represents what a family can accomplish when they take on a challenge. From the very beginning, my wife and I realized that the only chance our kids had to live independently was if we could get them to overcome their own limitations.

One common trait of autistic children is an unwillingness to try anything different, whether it was food or an activity. We recognized this early on when we noticed that our kids would prefer to eat only grapes and milk for the rest of their lives. I once heard someone compare autism to a warden, who keeps his subjects tucked away in an isolated cell, away from the rest of the world, providing only basic sustenance for their survival. Except with autism, there are no locks on the door as the inmates are perfectly content to serve out their life sentence.

At three years old, when we tried to transition my daughter Savannah into other drinks like juice, lemonade or even water, she absolutely refused all our attempts. Even force-feeding her water from a spill proof cup would only cause her to hold the tablespoon of water in her mouth for hours at a time before ultimately spitting the water out on the floor.

We met with our pediatrician and she noted that even autistic children have a survival instinct, and suggested that we withhold all milk until she was forced to drink something else just to quench her thirst. After three days of trying, we went back to the pediatrician because our daughter still had not relented and we were afraid she would pass out from sheer dehydration, although from all appearances she seemed fine.

It was only then that we figured out that she was supplementing her liquid intake with just enough grapes to enable her to stave off all our attempts to have her try something different.

From then on, we decided that the only solution would be for us to be as stubborn as our children until they realized that we would never give up. We started off slowly – instead of letting them eat the red grapes they were used to, we gave them green grapes. I would cajole, demand, and sometimes force the food into their mouths and badger them incessantly to swallow it. Even in restaurants, I would not make an exception, even though we often got some very unsympathetic stares from other customers as I was hovering around my screaming child who did not want to try a carrot.

Success came slowly, but gradually. They were equally resistant to vegetables as they were to cake and ice cream. After several weeks, they began to tolerate the new foods, and their objections slowly became less and less vocal.

After three years of this, our kids now eat just about everything, and enjoy it. My son Ethan eats peas, carrots, apples, and loves soup. Savannah is crazy about tofu, melons and oranges, although she's still not that wild on ice cream.

My wife and I are now disciplined enough to apply our version of "tough love" to nearly every aspect of their lives, whether we are trying to get them to speak, read and write, dress themselves, brush their teeth, or use the bathroom. Every improvement still begins with a struggle, but much less so as they know that Mom & Dad just aren't going to give up.

I know our approach may seem extreme to some, and we still have a long way to go. But for the first time, I often catch a glimpse of my son or daughter with a smile on their face after discovering something new and exciting for the very first time. The cell door is still unlocked, but for the first time, they'd actually like to open the door.

A Tour Guide of the Mundane

Each and every one of us, as San Diegans, shares a common bond. Perhaps more accurately, we share a common role. It is a role most of us assume with a sense of pride. It is a responsibility we all bear by living in America's Finest City.

You have chosen to reside in San Diego with all it has to offer, and by virtue of your decision you are now the *Quasi-official tour guide to all of your out of town friends and family.* When the barest of acquaintances calls to tell you they are coming to town, realize that you are what helped tip the scales in their minds when they couldn't decide between San Diego and Orlando.

Still, we take our hosting duties seriously because we all want to show off our city in the best possible light. Who wouldn't need to catch their breath when they first saw the dramatic cliffs off of La Jolla Cove? Who wouldn't be charmed by the romance of Hotel del Coronado? Who wouldn't want to try a fish taco?

I know all of San Diego's landmarks. Whether the guests are from Boston, Los Angeles or any point in between, I can arrange a whirlwind tour of local attractions and get them back on their plane headed home, happy and most importantly, out of my hair.

The challenge comes when I host guests from Asia. For these guests, I seem to enter an alternate universe where the attractions I take them to draw blank stares while they inadvertently stumble across a seemingly innocuous matter that ends up being the highlight of the trip.

As their tour guide, you start taking things personally. How would a tour guide feel if I traveled to Italy's Leaning Tower of Pisa and continuously admired at how straight and upright all the other buildings were? Or if I visited the Great Wall of China only to gush over how realistic the wall looked on the silk-screened T-shirts I bought at the gift stand?

I once took a family from Taiwan to an elegant Sunday brunch. They joked that this was the reason why Americans were overweight. On the other hand, when they found out how much they could save by buying vitamins in bulk, the amount they brought home could stamp out scurvy in several developing countries.

Then there was the time I took my father in law to visit Balboa Park to walk through all the beautiful gardens. Yet, when I asked him what he remembers of San Diego, he inevitably will say something like, "Oh…the hot dogs at Costco are so tasty and melt in your mouth."

When I visit Asia, you see how fast the pace can be. Crowds await you at every turn and everyone struggles through, day in and day out. You wonder whether their value system, like my own, might be influenced by what we experience in our own environments. Perhaps, for those who live life in a constant rush, a simple, solitary pleasure can be the most fulfilling.

Come to think of it, those hot dogs are pretty good.

Born Without a Funny Bone

I've lost my sense of humor.

It was just here a minute ago. I put it down for just a second while I was reaching for a snack, and then, suddenly - poof! It's gone.

This is a serious matter. Writing a humor column without a sense of humor can be a problem.

So that I might find my humor, I've decided to backtrack everything I've done over the last few hours to see if that might help jog my memory. Let's see…what have I been doing the last few hours?

8:00 pm: Decided to watch some television, maybe find a sitcom. Then I thought I'd like a snack and found a nice, tasty bag of cheese puffs. Nothing special on TV.

9:00 pm: Decided to give TV another chance, followed by a few more cheese puffs. Yuck, another show with people eating bugs. How disgusting. Wow, these cheese puffs are great.

10:00 pm: More TV. More puffs.

Hmm…

Wait a minute! Now I remember.

The truth is that I didn't lose my sense of humor. I've come to realize that I've never *had* a sense of humor.

I'm afraid it's even more serious than that. From what I can see, Asians in general don't have a sense of humor. We are not a funny group.

Now, you may ask, how did I come to this conclusion? I'm glad you asked.

Flipping through the channels, I'm suddenly aware that there are very few Asians on television, and practically none on any situation comedies. There's no "Everybody Loves the Chins", or "The Bernie Mah Show".

In a recent report by the *National Asian Pacific American legal Consortium*, their study shows that Asians play 2.7 percent of regular characters, with virtually no Asian actors on situation comedies. One network, CBS, had no Asian characters on any of their primetime shows.

Even on shows that owe much of their premise to Asian culture have little or no Asian representation on them. The hottest show on television today, "American Idol", which is essentially an extremely hyped up karaoke competition (which of course originated in Asia), has not had any major Asian singers in it's history. Unless, of course, you count William Hung, the famously off-key performer from a few years back (and please, let's *not* count William Hung).

I have to believe that the studio heads of ABC, CBS, NBC & Fox have done their due diligence to search far and wide for a comedy that could find humor in the lives of Asian Americans and have come up empty handed. They must have come to the same conclusion I have – Asians simply aren't very funny.

Of course, as an Asian humor writer, this disturbing conclusion has put a serious crimp in my style. I find myself frozen in self-doubt, uncertain that anything that I used to find funny is funny anymore.

For example:

When my uncle walks out of the bathroom with one end of a toilet paper roll stuck to his shoe and proceeds to walk down the hallway, out the front door, and halfway around the house while continuously unraveling the roll like a big long streamer – that's not funny.

When any of my non-Asian friends asks me about what I might know about any given news story that happens to take place in Asia and my standard response always begins with "Well, my sources tell me..." That's not funny.

When my uncle and father become so absorbed in their conversation while walking in a park that they simultaneously fall into a bush of rhododendrons – that's not funny.

When I once ask my six-year old son what he should do with all the food remaining on his plate when there were thousands of children in the world who were hungry and he replies, "Eat it real fast so they can't come here and steal it?" That's not funny.

When my parents decide to plan ahead and purchase adjoining plots in a memorial park and my father asks the park director about getting a "group discount" – that's not funny.

I suppose I'll have to look into a new profession. Maybe William Hung was on to something. I can see it now…Asian-American Idol.

Dazed and Confused in a Shopping Mall

I am currently writing this column from the food court of a shopping center in Las Vegas.

As an astute observer of human behavior, I feel compelled to share a revelation I just had while waiting in line for French fries, chili cheese hot dog and a "Moo-latte" cappuccino. I'm thinking that my discovery may bring countries and cultures closer together because it is a universal trait shared by all.

It turns out, after an enormous amount of research on my part, that no matter where you go, in whatever country or corner of the world that you happen to reside, that all shopping centers are exactly the same.

Unfortunately, I have a long way to go in proving my thesis. First of all, my wife Maya totally disagrees with me. It's possible that 50% of the world's population will disagree with me. However, it's also likely that the other 50%, many of whom are sitting next to me here in the food court babysitting a bevy of shopping bags dropped off by their significant other while they go back out to check the latest sale at "Casual Corner", well, they know what I mean.

I begin providing corroborating evidence to my wife by pointing out that nearly all the stores – Sunglass Hut, Ann Taylor, Wilson's Leather, the Gap, Coach, Cole Haan, etc., are all the same stores that you can find at any shopping center back home.

Then, I challenge her by asking, "Tell me what's different about this shopping mall compared to any other shopping mall we've ever been to back home."

Her response, which I'm afraid I cannot argue with, is "Well…this mall is completely different. First of all…um…well, it's in Vegas."

She's absolutely right. Another difference is that we didn't actually have to get on a plane, rent a car, and stay at a hotel to go to a shopping center back home. FYI - it's important to note that this was a distinction that I kept to myself, which is a tip I learned as an astute observer of human behavior as well being married for fourteen years.

Honestly though, shopping is something that relaxes Maya and she deserves whatever she wants if it helps her relax. After all, she is a savvy executive trainer that travels the world helping multinational companies. On the other hand, I'm savvy at eating cheetos using only my left hand so as not to contaminate the remote control in my other hand with excess cheese residue.

I'm sure there are some subtle differences from one shopping center to the next, and I suspect that they all seem the same to me because I have the same reaction every time we visit one. See if the following description rings true to all the men out there:

Upon entering a shopping center, time appears to stand still. People pass you by, going from store to store, without any concept of time. Unless of course, you see a "going out of business sale", in which case shoppers react as if they only had fifteen minutes left to purchase a Kate Spade handbag before the oncoming apocalypse.

For the most part, I walk around shopping centers in a daze, with a slightly confused look on my face. Should I spend the next hour sitting in the massage chair at The Sharper Image, or would I be better off buying a cinnamon twist pretzel at Auntie Ann's Soft Pretzels? I usually decide to splurge and end up eating a cinnamon twist pretzel while sitting in the Sharper Image massage chair.

It turns out that the vacant expression you see in men's faces while in a shopping mall is a diagnosable condition. I believe it's called "Shellshockedinamallitis". It's similar to a condition women get when they go with their husband or boyfriend to somewhere they want to go. I understand that condition is called "Dazedinacarshowitis."

A Complex Simplicity

As part of my research for this column, I watched an episode of Fox network's "The Simple Life" the other day. Let me re-emphasize that my sole purpose of watching the show was for research only, and not for the entertainment value. The fact that I own a "Honk if you want The Simple Life" bumper sticker or that I am an honorary member of the Paris Hilton Fan Club only goes to show how serious I am about my work.

The premise of "The Simple Life" is well, simple. It's the classic fish out of water tale. Place two young socialites in a rural setting like a farm, give them various tasks they are completely unfamiliar with (usually dealing with some farm animal), and watch the hilarity ensue.

The Simple Life. After watching the show, it dawned on me that this was part of a much greater phenomenon. I'm not referring so much to the show itself, but of the title. The simple life is something more and more of us aspire to. As our lives become more complex, with more demands on our time, who among us wouldn't rather experience the simple pleasure of milking a goat? Hmm…maybe that wasn't the best example.

You don't have to look hard to find people around you who have made a life choice to simplify their lives. I would bet that you know someone in your life who has given up a high paying job to open up a corner coffee shop, or drive an RV cross country, or even, live on a farm.

Each of us will find our own ways to uncomplicate our lives. I've decided that embracing technology is the way to go. Technology is designed to boost productivity, and reduce the amount of time for a given task. This also fits in perfectly with the fact that I am the ultimate gadget guy.

Don't believe me? On my desk where I am writing this column, I have two computers, two printers, a digital camera, a cell phone, a portable phone, a DVD burner, a scanner, an MP3 player, a VCR, a flat panel monitor, and three computer speakers. I'm typing this column with the keyboard on my lap as I have no room on my desk for anything else.

All right, I admit that as far as simplifying goes, I'm not off to the best start. But that's bound to change. After a thorough search process, I have identified the premier gadget that will have an enormous impact towards uncluttering my life. It's a cell phone, but beyond the features of the phone, it is also a digital day timer, a digital camera, video camera, voice recorder, e-mail center, MP3 player, and a calculator, all in one. For an extra $50, it comes with an attachment that will massage my back and make frozen yogurt.

The only thing is, you can't buy this product in the states yet. It's only available in Japan, and it'll be some time before it reaches here. But that's not really a problem for **Technoman** (I'm hoping people will start calling me that).

Unfortunately, these new products developed in Japan use only Japanese in the user's manuals and on the device itself. Still, I am determined to simplify my life. Therefore, as soon as I import this product from Japan and learn Japanese, my life will be uh…smooth sailing.

Hmm..let me get back to you.

The American Dream – Transplanted

The phone rings.

In my lonely hotel room in China, I was a bit surprised to get a call to my room. No one back home knew where I was staying, and I had just left my partner downstairs after a long day of work. It couldn't be him – he was as tired as I was and was probably even less inclined to talk "shop" any more.

Which left only one other possibility – my client, in the other room, must have a question for me.

"Wayne", he said, with a tinge of frustration, "I can't turn the lights on in my room."

"Oh, no problem." I said, mustering as much enthusiasm as I could. "Just take your card key and place it in the slot right inside your door. Then you can turn on the lights."

My client, the CEO of a large furniture company based in North Carolina, had never been to China before. In fact, I was surprised to find out that he had never been outside the U.S. before except for a short vacation in the Bahamas.

Given the situation, it was understandable that the whole "Card key in the slot to turn on the lights to help save energy" system most hotels in China use might, to my client, seem a bit, well…foreign.

The second call came a minute later.

"Wayne", he said, sounding more irate than before, "I punched the card in the slot, turned on the lights, went to take a shower, and in the middle of my shower all the lights turned off on me!"

"OK", I said, even more calmly than before. "Where is your card key?"

"It's on my dresser. Why?"

"Well, you have to leave the card key *in* the slot to keep the lights on."

The call ended with a bit of exasperation and a lot of good humor. Bridging two cultures as different as east and west, isn't too hard if you take it one small step at a time. That's the key – or in this case…the card key.

When traveling to China, it's amazing how much you discover about the various cultures as seen through the eyes of someone experiencing it for the first time. Much more so than when you experience it for the first time. My first visit to China was mostly a blur, just too much to digest. In this case, it was my CEO client, who I will call Frank, who was interested in finding some factories in China to build some new furniture lines for his company.

He had few preconceptions of what to expect. The ones he did have were negative, and were shaped primarily by what he heard on the news or read in the paper back home.

Chinese factories…sweatshops…child labor…substandard pay…dangerous work conditions – this was his fear. If that's what he found, he told me, his company would have no part of it.

I would never discount these stories. After all, China is a big country with an exploding economy. But that wasn't a part of the China I'd ever known or experienced.

Our first factory stop, in the industrial town of Dongguan, about a two-hour drive from Hong Kong, was in a furniture factory known for intricate hand carving.

As we arrived, we climbed out of our car and were greeted by the factory spokesperson, a young lady in her mid-twenties, named Lisa, who surprised us immediately with her English abilities. She had a strong command of the language, with a noticeable but pleasant accent. She spoke very succinctly, yet soft, in a very cordial way.

"Thank you for visiting our factory today." she said. "My name is Lisa and I am very honored to meet you. Let me take you on a tour of the facility and I would be most happy to answer any questions you might have."

We walked into a massive multi-story concrete building with large frosted windows on one side and loading docks on the other. Lisa led us through the first floor of the factory, quickly reeling off the various furniture tools they use to shape and assemble their products.

She stopped at one machine, a massive contraption with conveyer belts, monitoring screens and buttons too many to count. Lisa seemed to beam with pride as she drew her hand towards the machine. "This is a brand new sander we just purchased from a company in Germany.," she said. We bought it so our factory workers wouldn't have to sand nearly as much by hand and could increase productivity. We invested nearly $150,000 U.S. dollars on this machine."

Frank, who seemed right at home in this factory as it reminded him of his own factory back home, leaned over towards me with a big grin on his face, and whispered, "I've got two of those back home."

For Frank, nothing seemed out of the ordinary so far. It was a typical furniture factory, from the stacks of lumber lining the walls to the finished pieces drying in the finishing room. It wasn't until Lisa walked us upstairs that Frank's eyes began to widen.

At the top of the stairs, we entered a large room. There were over 100 factory people, both men and women, mostly in their 20's and 30's, sitting around large work benches lined up in rows across the room. They all seemed very slim, and wore mostly long sleeve shirts and pants, and seemed comfortable despite the hot, muggy weather.
As we walked past, you could hear the clickety-clack of hammers and chisels, carving into their work almost in unison, much like a symphony orchestra, but instead of music, they produced wood shavings, which covered the floor like confetti.

Lisa motioned to us to follow her. Stopping at one workbench with three women carving an intricate detail into what would end up being a sofa leg, Lisa said, "This is one of our carving rooms. We have two others on the premises that are much, much larger."

Frank, watching one young man carving at his station, called me over. He wanted me to ask the young man, who happened to be wearing a Michael Jordan T-shirt, some questions, out of earshot from Lisa, to get an unvarnished response.

In my broken Chinese, I did my best to start a conversation.

"How are you?" I asked, "Could you tell me how long you've worked here?"

The young man, looking surprised that we had approached him, said, "I've been working here for eight years. I have been carving for five years."

"Are you from Dongguan?" I asked.

"No, my family lives very far, far away, in the country."

"How did you find a job here?"

"I was very fortunate. This factory is in a special administrative zone. I came here to look for work and I had to apply for a permit so that I could work here. I make enough to send money back home to take care of my parents and family."

Frank, unable to understand a word of our conversation, pointed at the young man's T-shirt, smiled and said, "Do you like Michael Jordan?"

The worker looked up, eyes beaming, and proudly exclaimed, "Chee-ca-go Bullsah!"

A few minutes later, a loud alarm rang and all the workers quietly filed out of the factory into the large courtyard outside.

"It's lunchtime," Lisa said. "I think they are having stewed chicken on rice today. Would you like to see?"

Walking downstairs into the courtyard, we see all the factory workers waiting single file in a line snaking around the building leading to the lunch counter. Along the way, Frank began asking Lisa many more questions.

How much do they make, on average? Do you take care of their food and housing? How often do they get to go home?
Lisa explained that the factory provides food and housing, and that the factory shuts down several weeks a year to allow the workers to go home to family. She said that the average pay for a factory worker was $60 to $70 U.S. dollars a week, but that was about four times what they could make back in their hometown.

Finishing our visit, Lisa walked us to our car and wished us well.

For the rest of the week, we continued to visit factory after factory. Some factories specialize in painting, some in metal work, and others in glass making.

At the end of the week, as we shuffled back into the car for the long drive back to Hong Kong, Frank gazed out the window, and spoke, almost to himself.

"You know what surprised me about this week?" he asked, not really expecting me to answer. "These are very hard working people, who seem to feel very fortunate that they've found work here. They're taking care of their families, and seem very proud that they have found something productive to do. You don't always see that back home nowadays."

When I come back home, I inevitably read stories about how Wal-Mart is destroying our domestic manufacturing industry by importing inexpensive products from China or how India is stealing engineering contracts from local companies who can't compete with their lower wages. When I do, I think back about that trip I had with Frank.

As an American, I can understand the frustration of people who have lost their job to someone unknown from a far away land. Yet, as difficult as that is, I also understand that a global economy is simply that – global. The person finding that job didn't do it out of spite against us, they did it so that they could take care of their family, just as we would like to do for ours.

I don't pretend to have the solution. I doubt setting up artificial trade barriers or tariffs against China will work unless we set them up against Vietnam, Thailand, Mexico and any other country that has significantly lower wages than us, which seems impractical.

While we will never be able to compete in competitive wages, in the end it may boil down to American ingenuity, an area in which our country excels and to this day, has no equal.

In that respect, the American dream is alive and well.

The Michael Jordan of Sons

My son will be the Tiger Woods of tennis. No, even better, he will be the Michael Jordan of tennis. Wait, wait, my son will be the next Andre Agassi of uhh….well, tennis.

At least that's my fantasy.

There comes a point in fatherhood where most Dads, foist all his hopes, dreams, and aspirations on his kid. In my case, I have my ten-year-old son, Tyler.

I think this generational rite of passage starts from a biological urge for fathers to transfer every ounce of ambition and unfulfilled aspiration into their son so that we can live vicariously through them. It's bred into us. We can't help ourselves. I believe the clinical term for the condition is "Needtopassthebuckology".

I see signs of it every time I get together with my friends. "My son just got an all-star award delivered to our home for baseball!" said one. My other friend called up to tell me that he's started coaching his two boys in junior tennis and that one of his boys was characterized as being especially gifted.

In fact, now that I think of it, every one of my friends who has a son who is at least eight years old has told me that their son is especially gifted in one sport or another. I have yet to meet a father who has an average or "gift-less" child.

All of this, of course, only intensifies my obsession to discover the super human-like talent that must lie somewhere within Tyler. If all these other so-called gifted boys are that good, then surely Tyler must possess the kind of Schwarzenegger-like strength and cheetah-like reflexes to excel in any sport.

I figured, once we discovered Tyler's athletic gifts, in short order we could expect opponents to fall to their knees in dejection once they saw the phenomenon that is Tyler and realize that any attempt to compete against him was basically a futile delay of the inevitability of his unstoppable awesomeness.

Perhaps my expectations were a tad high.

I've taken him out to the tennis court, since I'm a pretty good player and I figured it was a good place to start. I taught him the basics, and he gets excited when he hits the ball and gets a little frustrated when he misses. He is fine when we are on the court, but you distinctly get the feeling he would be just as happy riding his bike or goofing off with his friends.

He has no obsession for the game, and based on my experience with him, the same goes for soccer, baseball, or any other organized sport. As a dad who loves his son, I've come to realize that whatever he does, as long as he tries, is fine with me.

So, after a few weeks of coming to this conclusion, I was pleasantly surprised yesterday that Tyler wanted me to take him out to the tennis court and hit some balls.

Of course, with my outlandish expectations once again quickly re-established, I readily obliged and we headed to the courts.

On the court, Tyler ran around, trying to hit every shot, including ones he couldn't realistically reach. He kept at it, and only took a break just to get some water. We played for 90 minutes and for the first time, he seemed to revel in the game.

Time to work on those sponsorship deals again.

Once we were done, we came home and he wanted to get some more water. He opened up the refrigerator, and all at once, one of the side drawers fell off and a number of glass jars burst on the floor. Tyler looked a bit stunned, and I told him to step away from the broken glass but that it was OK and that these things happen sometimes. Yet, he looked dejected.

I told him, "It's OK, Tyler. It's just an accident. I'm not mad at you." He said, "I just wanted this to be a perfect day, and now you have to clean up this mess."

Not quite understanding what he meant, I asked him, "What do you mean you wanted this to be a perfect day?" He said, "You know, the card I gave you this morning, you and I spending time together today."

Then I realized what my ten year old meant. That morning, he gave me a card. For the last few years on that day, he's given me a card. A father's day card. And now I realized, he played his heart out on the tennis court on that day…for me.

At least for me, it was the best father's day a father could ask for.

The Dog Days of 2006

As we are soon approaching Chinese New Year, I thought it would be appropriate to do a little research so that I might be able to impart some words of wisdom on this festive occasion.

As you may know, every Chinese New Year celebrates a specific animal. There are twelve animals in the cycle, and at the end of the cycle you start all over again. Some of the animals in the cycle include the rat, the snake, and the goat (or Ram).

This year, it turns out, is the year of the dog. As luck would have it, we actually own a dog. Therefore, for the benefit of my readers, I have been observing the behavior of our dog "Bingo" for the last few days.

In addition, in order to bolster my findings, I looked up a few interesting factoids on various personality traits associated with the year of the dog.

Herewith, are my findings, in the form of a true/false test on how well these traits matched up with what I observed in my dog Bingo:

Trait Number One: Those who fall under the Year of the Dog have a deep sense of loyalty and inspire confidence in others because they keep secrets well.

This is TRUE. A few days ago while I was home alone with only Bingo as my companion, I decided to polish off the last of the leftover birthday cake from a party earlier in the week despite my wife's threats of hiring a nutritionist to follow me around if I ate it. When my wife got home, my loyal dog not only kept his mouth shut, but he didn't even bat an eye when I tried to blame him for eating the cake.

I bet that if I owned a rat or a goat for a pet that they would have spilled the beans the second my wife walked through the door.

Trait Number Two: They care little for wealth; yet somehow always seem to have money.

This is TRUE. While I am sure that Bingo has never held down a paying job, somehow a package gets mailed to us every couple of weeks containing doggie treats, milk bones, and the latest issue of "Dog Fancy" magazine.

Trait Number Three: They are eccentric, somewhat selfish, and terribly stubborn.

This is INCONCLUSIVE. While it is true that Bingo does exhibit some odd behavior (anyone who has seen where he likes to scratch himself knows what I'm talking about), it is false that he is selfish because he will generously drop any dead rodent he has caught at my feet as he comes in from the backyard.

Trait Number Four: They can be cold and emotionally distant at parties.

This is FALSE. Call it what you will, but after seeing what Bingo did on my neighbor's leg the last time he visited, the last words you would use to describe his behavior is "cold and emotionally distant."

Where is that dog anyways? I need him. There's a pastrami sandwich in the refrigerator with my name on it.

Hogging Up All The Attention For Chinese New Year

I have a dilemma.

I've been asked to devote this column to the upcoming Chinese New Year, which for 2007 celebrates the Year of the Pig. The only problem is that I'm having a tough time with the subject matter.

It's not that I can't think of anything to say – on the contrary, I've got loads of material. My problem is that as a humor writer, I am having a hard time resisting the temptation to throw out pithy little pork-related zingers as I try to write something serious in commemoration of this year's honored animal, the pig. I mean - I could really go hog-wild.

You see - it's starting already.

I just find it especially hard to write about this year's guest of honor whose closest connection to me were the sausage links I had for breakfast this morning.

Shoot. You see? I just can't help myself.

I need to be able to put aside my own western notions of what a pig represents and try to understand the inner beauty of this esteemed animal. From what I've read, the pig of Chinese astrology is perhaps the most generous and kind of all the animals. Pigs are down to earth, caring of friends, and completely selfless.

According to Astrology.com, pigs "...are so magnanimous they can appear almost saintly. (They are) highly intelligent creatures, forever studying, playing and probing in their quest for greater knowledge. They can be misinterpreted as being lazy however, due to their love of napping, taking long bubble baths or dallying over an incredible spread of rich foods."

Magnanimous and saintly? Quest for greater knowledge? Taking long bubble baths or dallying over an incredible spread of rich foods? Am I missing something? We are talking about a pig and not a Nobel Prize-winning, recently ordained pastor/super-model, right?

Oops, there I go again. I'm letting my western bias' slip through. Well, at least I've managed to get through this much of the column without using the word "bacon" a single time.

Blast it.

This darned pig is obviously making it hard for me to reconcile between my Asian heritage and my American upbringing. Does it have to be a pig? Why not a more acceptable animal, like a swan? Why can't we have the Year of the Swan? I can write my tail off waxing poetic about the elegance and beauty of a swan.

A swan won't work? Fine, how about the Year of the Eagle, or the Year of the Giraffe? How about the Year of the Gazelle? I can do a moose, a beaver, a porcupine…no problem. I just don't think I can do a pig justice.

Is this whole Chinese Zodiac animal system written in stone or is anyone taking suggestions?

While we're at it, can someone please explain how we can have the year of the snake, monkey, and rooster but the CHINESE New Year celebration doesn't have a Year of the Panda? How can that possibly be?

The Year of the Pig. I'm sorry - I'm just not up to the challenge. I'm stuck. I'm completely hog-tied.

I know - you saw that one coming.

Well, it's only a year. Maybe next year's animal will be a better fit for me. Let's see here, 2008 is the year of the…rat.

Someone help me.

The Year of the Adorable Rodent

I've been asked to write a column celebrating this year's Chinese New Year. As with other columns celebrating the New Year, I thought a festive poem might be in order. Unfortunately, I'm having some problems with it.

My main concern (and I could see it coming), is that I'm having a hard time waxing poetic about the animal we are celebrating this year.

You see, this year is the year of the rat.

To give the rat it's due, I did some research and the rat is highly regarded in its place in the Chinese Zodiac. The rat is active, pleasant, and quick to see opportunities. They are sociable, family minded…and able to withstand global thermonuclear explosions.

OK, I threw that last part in, and therein lies my problem. Wait, instead of explaining it, why don't I just show you the poem. I call it, "Ode to Rat".

Ode to Rat, by Wayne Chan

Oh, blessed rat, so misunderstood,
One thing to avoid, I know I would
You scuttle away, scampering here and there,
With your long bare tail, and scrubby gray hair

You're honored this year, and while that might seem screwy,
You weren't half bad in the film "Ratatouille".
Perhaps there's more to you, than pestilence and fleas,
After all, you do have a penchant for a nice fine cheese.

They say at a party, you're the center of attention,
How you end up being invited, is beyond comprehension.
They say that beauty is only skin deep,
Yet from what I've seen, that's a pretty big leap.

So here we are, in the year of the Rat.
And from what I've been told, you really are all that.

I'll give you your props, but I don't want to be vague,
This may be your year, just don't give us the plague.

This is not exactly a poem I'd likely submit to the Readers Digest, if you know what I mean.

I'm not sure, but it might be the first time that anyone has ever incorporated the words "pestilence" and "plague" in a poem.

Seriously though, as with every New Year, it's a time to appreciate what you have in your life and to look forward to the blessings of a new year. Happy New Year to you and your family, and may a year of health and happiness be right around the corner.

From Noodles to Burgers & Back

I am witnessing a metamorphosis.

Like millions of other Chinese Americans, I grew up in a family where my parents were born and raised in China. They moved to the United States to find a better life and it was also where they met, fell in love, got married, and ultimately had me – their most "cherished and prized progeny".

OK, maybe I've never heard them use the term "cherished and prized progeny", but I digress. Let me get back to my point.

The point is, both my parents completely embraced the ideal that America was the grand social experiment, the place where the diversity of America is part of our national identity. It is the place where we would be both Chinese and American.

Despite having to learn English and the intricacies of Western culture, both my parents excelled in what they set out to do. My mother started out as a nurse before becoming the head of a library in a major University. Likewise, my father started out as a professor of Electrical Engineering at a University before starting several successful businesses.

Without forgetting their culture or values, they embraced Western culture. We rooted for our favorite football team every Sunday. We bought a station wagon with faux wood paneling on the side of it and went for rides on Saturday afternoons with no particular destination. On weekends, Dad would roast a whole side of beef just to feed the four of us.

If America ever had a melting pot, our family was swimming in the deep end.

Nowadays, my Mom is retired and my Dad is semi-retired. Yet, it has come as somewhat of a surprise to see the transformation I've observed over at my parent's house over the last couple of years.

It started out slowly, when I noticed that the coffee table in the family room started getting stacked with piles of Chinese newspapers. Then I started noticing that nearly every evening that I dropped by, one or both of them were watching Chinese soap operas. The next thing you know, Mom and Dad cancelled their opera tickets and have become aficionados of Lang Lang, the Chinese pianist who plays mainly Chinese music.

This last week, despite the fact that Mom knows virtually nothing about computers or networking, she managed to install an internet service that connects to their TV and allows them to get Chinese programming direct from China and Taiwan.

What is going on here? It's as if the melting pot is no longer stirring and all the ingredients have decided to "go their own way". If America's acculturation really is a grand experiment, apparently my parents have decided to "revert to their original state".

Don't get me wrong. I'm as proud as anyone of my Chinese heritage, and I've spent the last 25 years trying to understand where I came from and the history behind it. But, they brought me up in this country (Refer to "Cherished and prized progeny" above) and raised me to value both sides of my cultural identity. I don't like seeing either side getting short shrift.

For a little while, I thought that I might need to alter my behavior to keep things in balance. Perhaps I could spend a little time savoring various aspects of Americana as the "yin" to the "yang" of my parent's recent "re-calibration" to their roots.

I would do this by going on a road trip, driving a Chevy pickup, visiting various baseball stadiums on my way to Cleveland's Rock and Roll Hall of fame while only listening to CD's of Woody Guthrie and stopping to eat only at roadside diners that served hamburgers, chocolate malts and apple pie.

In the end, I decided not to make the trip. First of all, it's nearly impossible to find someone who will rent you a Bassett hound for a road trip, and secondly (and most importantly), I realized that even with all the Chinese videos and newspapers they have accrued, Mom and Dad remain quintessentially Chinese-American.

How do I know this? Easy.

Look at where they decided to live their lives.

The Anti-Asian Stereotype Man

With all the turbulence and activity in California reaching a fever pitch in recent weeks, I have decided that as a Californian, I must do whatever I can to give back to this great state that has given me so much. In my own small way, I will contribute to this cause by assuming a role I was born to play and am ready to assume.

In case you're still in the dark as to what my decision is, let me be perfectly clear. I hereby announce my plan to be the next movie blockbuster action/adventure hero.

Governor? No, no, no, no no. There are enough people running for that already. Still, the California's recall election did give me the idea for this sudden career change.

After all, for the time being, Arnold is taking a leave of absence from his action/adventure hero duties, and Sylvester, Bruce, and Clint are getting a bit long in the tooth for some of the action stunts that are part of this genre. My time has come.

Some of you may ask, "Wayne, I just don't see you as an action/adventure hero and besides, aren't there already several Asian actors who are doing quite well?"

You mean like Jackie Chan, Jet Li and Chow Yun Fat? That's a fair question, but I believe I can fill a special niche that these fine actors cannot. Let me try and describe my action/adventure hero persona.

First off, I intend to be the first Asian action/adventure star with no martial art skills whatsoever. When a bad guy tries to hit me, they'll succeed. However, like in Arnold and Sylvester's movies, when it looks like I'm down for the count with the fate of the world on my shoulders, I will somehow manage to head butt them which will leave my opponent completely stunned but apparently causes me no discomfort whatsoever.

If that doesn't work and my adversary has me over a barrel, somehow, somewaym I will conveniently find something like a crow bar within arms reach that I can use to break free or possibly some kind of mechanical lever that when pulled will suck my enemy into some ridiculously dangerous mechanical contraption.

I have a cousin who has managed to land a few bit parts in movies and the types of roles he's played might serve as a guideline of what I am trying to avoid. He has played the son of an Asian crime lord who is snuffed out before the end of the opening credits. He has played a clumsy Chinese waiter who is snuffed out before the end of the opening credits. Then of course there was what would have been his "breakthrough" role (which ultimately ended up on the cutting room floor in order to save room for the opening credits).

If that doesn't work, I still have plenty of options. But if it does, my new career as an action/adventure star is just a stepping stone to my real dream – just think of it…Senator Wayne Chan.

Turning Nothing Into a Political Career

I must admit that I am a political junkie. If it weren't for the kids, work, my wife, and her insistence that I take a shower **every** single day...I could watch the evening news shows indefinitely.

I get a kick out of watching the verbal sparring, the veiled insults, the accusations that are thrown about and then denied the following day – and that's just from the political pundits.

Our democratic process is often messy, but it's something we have all come to expect, coming from the world's oldest democracy. I wouldn't trade if for anything else, and it comes as no surprise then, that in other, younger democracies, the process can get downright scary.

I've watched clips of the Taiwanese legislature get so heated that actual fights have broken out in session – sometimes between men and women. In one session, I saw shoes being thrown between legislators. There were penny loafers, wing-tips, pumps, and stilettos – projectiles launched at a high rate of speed. I haven't seen so many shoes tossed about since the last time Nordstrom Rack had it's semi-annual sale.

I checked Taiwan's constitution and under Article 11, it states, *"The people shall have freedom of speech, teaching, writing, and publication."* I double-checked to make sure no one had added an addendum like *"...but if you disagree with what someone has said, feel free to fling your footwear in protest."*

Back in the U.S., it occurred to me that if the current vetting process is good enough to elect someone as important as a president, wouldn't that same process be just as reliable in making some of our everyday decisions?

To test my theory, I decided to try out this strategy while interviewing someone who was interested in being our babysitter.

The following interview took place between the baby sitter, (or in more politically correct terms, the PALF, which stands for: Pre-Adult Life-skills Facilitator) and me.

ME: *Thanks so much for coming down to see us. Tell us why you'd like to be our PALF?*

PALF: *Well, I love children, and I find it rewarding to take care of kids.*

ME: *I see here that you used to be a Girl Scout and you've won some awards for selling the most cookies.*

PALF: *Yes, sir.*

ME: *Were you aware that cookies in general are loaded with carbs and sugar and if consumed regularly and in large quantities could play an adverse role in our children's future obesity and hypertension problems? Why would you, someone who claims to love children, intentionally encourage behavior that effects our kids lives, and by extension, the lives of a future generation of kids?*

PALF: *Sir?*

ME: *What I need to know now, and what I think our kids have a right to know, is whether their PALF is Pro-Health or Pro-Snack?*

PALF: *Sir! Of course, I want all kids to be healthy but…!*

ME: *Why the evasiveness, PALF? Next topic – I have a picture of you and a friend standing in front of what appears to be an Eminem concert, is this true? Is it? Is it? **I need an answer!***

I immediately end the interview as I see her take off her shoes.

To Golf Or Not To Golf
...That Is The Problem

I work in an industry where hard work pays off. If you apply yourself, learn your trade, plan ahead, and work with people in a professional way and customers with great respect, you may just have a chance to move your way up the professional ladder.

Or, you can just learn how to play golf.

I don't know how many times I've heard of non-golfers complaining that they've poured their soul into a proposal, sleekly integrating elaborate spreadsheets and color schematics, only to have it reviewed and critiqued over and over again, while two people playing a round of golf can iron out a multi-year agreement before the 9th hole with the contract sketched out in pencil on the back of a scorecard.

Of course, I've learned that golf plays a role in nearly any type of professional business. But in my industry, where I help multi-national companies work in Asia, golf is viewed as a near religion. In Asia, where open space is relatively limited, a membership to an exclusive golf course in, for example, Hong Kong, can run several hundred thousand dollars, and there's a waiting list to get in.

As for myself, I'm not a complete beginner, but in my lifetime, I've tried the game. It's not for me. I'm not very good. I don't see the point. I don't like wearing funny pants.

If I had to choose between playing golf or, say, watching bread rise, it's pretty much a toss up for me. Unless, of course, they were baking a nice fluffy egg bread, which I can never resist.

Still, if the simple act of playing golf is going to help my career, who am I to question it?

So, while on a trip to South China a few weeks ago and the opportunity presented itself, I told my partners, "Sure, let's do it! Show me those funny pants!"

For the benefit of all my fellow non-duffers out there, I'd like to share my experience playing a round of golf in Dongguan China. I've summarized these helpful hints into a report I call, "Five rules to playing a round of golf."

Rule #1: When someone asks you what your handicap is, don't respond by describing a recent mishap when you accidentally fell down the stairs. They're asking you something entirely different.

Rule #2: You cannot have enough golf balls. Think of how many golf balls a normal person would use, and then triple it. Be sure to buy golf balls at a sporting goods store and not at the pro shop at the course. I have a strong suspicion that the golf balls sold in the pro shops are coated with some type of magnetic resin so as to make them highly attractive to sand pits, trees and any body of water within a ten mile radius.

Rule #3: When one of your group is set to tee-off and is in the middle of their swing, don't answer a call on your cell phone by shouting, "Well, how the heck are ya!" unless you are wearing a lot of padding to protect yourself from flying golf clubs.

Rule #4: As you are ready to tee off, keep your head down, bend at the knees, gently grip your club, remember to pivot your weight from your back leg to the front, and strike the ball cleanly as you smoothly stroke the ball and continue with a natural follow through.

After the ball dribbles off to the bushes to your side, be sure to blame it on some kind of medical condition that prevented you from a "full extension." Find some malady that people have heard of but don't know well enough to ask you any specific questions about. During my round, I had a severe bout of "lumbago".

Rule #5: If your skill levels are like mine, and if you don't have a caddy, you will have no idea which club to use at any given time. Watching which club your partners are using would be helpful, except for the fact that since they are better than you, they are usually 100 yards ahead of you and you won't have any high powered binoculars that would allow you to see which club they are using.

Instead, I've found it very useful to select a club based on whatever is your lucky number. Since eight is my lucky number, I naturally pull out my eight iron. As your partners are busy taking their shots, with the club in your left hand, pick up your ball with your right hand and heave it as hard as you can toward the green. Since your partners won't have a high powered binocular to see what you just did…well, you get the picture.

The only problem is, my golf partners were always so far away from me that I never had the opportunity to talk about any business.

Note: A very decent and honorable friend of mine has been going through some health problems recently. When we both worked at the same company, he showed me the ropes and was always willing to lend a helping hand. Golf was and is his passion, and I'd like to dedicate this column to him. Sammy, all your friends wish you a speedy recovery.

Justice In The Name Of Purple

I was channel surfing the other day and decided to do my civic duty and watch one of the recent presidential debates that was on. Besides, there weren't any reruns of Seinfeld on so...

At one point during the debate, one of the candidates used an oft-used phrase, which I find puzzling and a little annoying. The line comes up whenever diversity issues are addressed and usually sounds something like this:

As an American, it shouldn't matter whether you are black, white, brown, red, yellow, or purple, everyone deserves an equal chance.

Now, I know which groups they are referring to and it doesn't take too much insight to know that "yellow" represents Asians.

For me, that statement always begs the question: Who are these purple people and why are Asians always grouped next to them?

Have I been so isolated in my life that I have overlooked an entire population of people in need of protection? Are Asians always grouped next to them because as an ethnic group, we are also often overlooked as a population? Where are all the purple people in my neighborhood? Am I losing my mind?

Then, quick as a flash, it comes to me. I know who this group is. It was right under my nose the whole time, and what's more, this purple group is one of the most maligned segments in the country. The worst part of it is, I have been one of the biggest offenders.

Of course I am referring to – Barney the dinosaur. But the purple population includes not only Barney, but all of the robotically trained kids that surround him as well.

I must confess, like many others, I loathe Barney. I can't explain it. Perhaps it's a visceral response to the whole Barney "package". You watch Barney, and you think that no being, human or animal, in this world or beyond, at any time since creation, could be so nauseatingly sweet without having to suffer through a terminal gag reflex.

Mercifully, we only have one Barney video, which I believe was given to my kids as a present (By the way, whoever gave it to us, mark my words – I am going to hunt you down). The highlight of the video is a song where Barney teaches kids to cover their mouth when they sneeze. For good measure, they bring in some kids who used to appear with Barney years ago, and they sing and dance their hearts out – all in honor of the sneeze. By the end of the video, I'm usually scratching my fingernails across a blackboard just trying to drown out the noise of the song.

Maybe it's because everyone seems so enchanted by a song about oral hygiene. Perhaps it's because some of these older kids prancing around look like they're pushing 40.

Well, it's time for a change. After all, who am I to judge? It's time for a fresh start. After all, it shouldn't matter whether you are black, white, brown, red, yellow or...

General Tso – Your Check is in the Mail

When the word, "genius" is used in normal, every day conversation, it is often used to describe the accomplishments of someone noteworthy. You've got Albert Einstein and the theory of relativity, Thomas Edison and the invention of the light bulb, and George Crum, the inventor of the potato chip. Who would ever think of questioning their respective contributions to society?

For me, a genius is someone whose accomplishment stands out not necessarily because of how earth shattering their achievement is to society, but rather in the way that their achievement inconspicuously creeps into the fabric of every day life. For a good example of this, please refer back to Mr. Crum and his potato chip.

So who would personify my definition of a true genius? General Tso T'sung-t'ang, inventor (or inspiration) for General Tso's chicken.

According to *The Harper Encyclopedia of Military Biography*, General Tso was born in Hunan, China and lived from 1812 to 1885. He joined Hunan's military in 1853 and became a full-fledged general by 1860. During his military career, he was most well known for his leadership in driving out the Taiping rebels from Hunan despite being hopelessly outnumbered. He went on to become a governor of the Chekiang province, and later a secretary of state. He died in Foochow on September 5, 1885, and was considered by many to be a hero.

Did you notice in the above description that there was no mention of General Tso actually coming up with his chicken dish? In my research of General Tso, at no point did I see any mention of his culinary skills. I never heard any quote from him saying, "You know what? Before the Taiping rebels arrive, I've just got to tell you about this chicken dish I came up with the other day."

In fact, in my research, I found General Tso's name to be spelled in any number of ways, from Tzo, Cho, Chau, Tao, and several other variations. The correct pronunciation of his name ran the gamut as well, although most seemed to agree that it was pronounced, "Sow", rhyming with "cow".

Upon further investigation, it is quite possible that General Tso had nothing to do with this chicken dish, and that it was more likely invented in a Chinese restaurant in New York in the 1970's. Furthermore, "General Tso's Chicken" is not really even an authentic Chinese entrée, since it is not a dish you will ever find in China. Finally, in the few times I've tried it at different Chinese restaurants, it always comes out a different way – sometimes sweet, sometimes salty, and sometimes spicy. The only common denominator that I came up with was that the prime ingredient was thankfully, chicken.

So what you end up with is a faux Chinese dish that is listed on every Chinese menu in America, usually in the more expensive "Chef's Specialties" section, misspelled and mispronounced a hundred different ways after a long dead Hunan general who had nothing to do whatsoever with the dish that was named after him, and tastes completely different every time you order it.

Call me crazy, but that's genius.

My only quibble is that as far as I know, neither General Tso nor any of his descendents ever benefited financially from his ubiquitous recipe. I guess this was before the time of Mrs. Fields Cookies, Orville Redenbacher's popcorn, or even General Tso's modern day counterpart, Colonel Sander's Kentucky Fried Chicken.

It makes you wonder if George Crum ever got any residuals from all those potato chips.

Maybe We Could Create a Dessert Called TIR-AH-MAH-SU

After exhaustive research at restaurants here and abroad I can confidently proclaim that the tradition of serving fortune cookies at the end of a Chinese meal is a custom found only in the United States and nowhere in Asia.

When traveling abroad, if you ask for a fortune cookie in an Asian restaurant, the servers don't seem to comprehend the question, as if it's a completely foreign topic to them (which, of course, it is). I may as well be asking the server, "Yes, and after the last dish, would you mind if I brought in my pet sheep so that we could play a few rounds of canasta?"

It is not commonly known that all newly arrived immigrants from China interested in starting Chinese restaurants here in the States must first attend a fortune cookie orientation course covering topics including: 1) Fortunes addressing general topics like health and wealth are appropriate; more specific information related to cholesterol levels and alimony are not, and 2) Customers believe that the lottery numbers printed on the back side of the fortune have been personally vetted by a wise old man channeling his predictions from a lotto picking Buddha.

The practice of customers getting a free dessert seems unique to Chinese restaurants. I've tried the whole "free dessert" concept at other restaurants without much luck. I was once asked to leave an Italian restaurant when I insisted that they serve me a complimentary cannelloni for dessert.

It makes common sense that the fortune cookie was created in the U.S. Americans place a much higher emphasis on desserts than Asians do.

The easiest way to see this is in what foods are presented at various cuisines. Japanese restaurants have bright bars set up with hundreds of pictures of sushi that can be created at a moment's notice. Spanish restaurants also have "bars", serving a varied assortment of "tapas", small dishes with a wide range of flavors, certain to please. Of course, Chinese restaurants serve "dim sum", which are small appetizer-sized dishes served from a steamy cart pushed around the restaurant, with the sight and smell of the dishes guaranteed to find it's owner in short time. These examples are for the most part, main entrees.

I can't recall ever going to an American restaurant and having the server bring out a tray of main entrees for me to select from. You certainly won't see him describing each entrée on the tray either ("As you can see, tonight we have a delectable meat loaf, served with brown gravy and mashed potatoes, or perhaps tonight you are more in the mood for our signature dish, we call it 'pot roast'".

Which brings me back to desserts. Restaurants in the west have "The Dessert Tray". This is the tray the server will inevitably bring to your table to tempt you with the most outrageous concoctions known to man. My favorite is the "Flourless chocolate torte with chocolate chips covered with a chocolaty-chocolate sauce."

The dessert tray won my family over long ago. Just last week, as the dessert tray arrived at our table, my son started gasping for air, looking weak. When I asked him what was wrong, he said, "Can't breathe…don't know if I'm going to make it…must…have…chocolate cake."

A Home of Good Fortune and Little Patience

I have always been struck by the stark contrasts between rationality versus spirituality in Asian culture. On the one hand, as typified by my father, you have the rational – an electrical engineer who sees everything at face value. He believes that whatever "luck" he has had in life came upon him by virtue of hard work. My dad will resole his old shoes when they become worn not because he doesn't want to spend the money on new shoes, but because there's nothing wrong with the rest of the shoe.

On the other hand, as typified by one of my favorite aunts, you have the spiritual. She believes that there are spirits and forces among us, good and bad, that can influence our lives for better or worse. In my youth, I can recall many instances where she would describe how to attract good luck while warding off evil spirits. She once told me that when eating a steamed whole fish, it was bad luck to eat every morsel of the fish because having leftover fish will invite good fortune to return. I only wish she had mentioned that a little earlier in the meal.

I would tend to be 99% rational, 1% spiritual. I believe that one's life is a result of choices made. On the other hand, I don't think it hurts to leave a little fish on the plate.

This contrast became abundantly clear as my wife Maya and I started looking for a new house. Let me say that Maya works amazingly hard managing home and career, but she also believes in Feng Shui, which literally means "Wind/Water", and is a methodology meant to attract positive energies, often times through the design and position of one's home.

I would say Maya is 75% rational, and 75% spiritual. (Don't bother doing the math, I was never very good at statistics).

We hired a well-respected feng shui master to do a reading of several homes we were interested in. He looked through various room layouts, analyzing the positive and negative aspects of each design.

In order to be a supportive hubby, I was determined to be open-minded. I was sure the spiritual aspect of feng shui could work in harmony with the rational needs we had of our future home.

The type of homes we liked were one-story ranch homes, usually with a courtyard near the front door, with the kid's rooms on one side of the house and the master bedroom on the other. If we needed to add a window here or hang a mirror there, that was fine with me. That's the least a supportive, open-minded hubby could do.

After spending five minutes going through the room layouts, the feng shui master made the following observations.

1. Having a courtyard near the front door at the center of a house was inappropriate symbolically because it was akin to having an empty heart.
2. Having too many rooms on one side of the house created an imbalance, which would create an imbalance in our lives.
3. To improve balance, instead of a long, ranch style home, we would be better off with a two story, square-shaped house.

Upon leaving the feng shui master, I may have inadvertently muttered something like, "Well, why don't we just buy a house in the shape of a toaster and be done with it?"

Bad, bad, closed-minded, skeptical hubby. Perhaps the feng shui master was right – we were already channeling negative energies. Unfortunately, the negative vibes were all emanating from my mouth.

To Beard or not to Beard

Halloween is a time where we can act out some of our fantasies and be rewarded with candy for doing so. Now that my kids are at an age where they appreciate Halloween, I find myself experiencing the same sense of fun and excitement through their eyes.

But, for the longest time, Halloween has been a reminder of a painful memory. The memory of a day, years ago, when I realized that the sky was not the limit and that everything was not possible.

The thing is - I cannot grow a beard. Hello, my name is Wayne Chan, and I have stubble envy.

I am talking about my inability to let have that rugged unshaven look, and don't even get me started about a full on beard. I am not unlike most Asians in that respect.

Why is it such a big deal, you say?

I recall countless movies where the hero goes out to the wilderness to save the day and they all seem to have stubble by the time they get there. Remember Harrison Ford in the Indiana Jones movies? Major stubble. Don Johnson in Miami Vice? Stubble city. Even when James Bond gets thrown out of an airplane wearing a tuxedo, he somehow manages to land safely on the ground, tuxedo intact, yet somehow during the fall is able to grow a five o'clock shadow.

I like to be clean-shaven for business. For meetings, I'm "clean-shaven, professional sales guy". But on weekends, if I ever go out to the forest (and it doesn't matter that I never do), I want to be "Rough and tumble stubble guy." Instead, I look like "clean-shaven, professional sales guy" in the forest.

It's not like I haven't tried to grow a beard. The problem is that I only grow a significant amount of hair right under my chin and it grows out long and straggly. After a couple weeks, I look less like "Rough and tumble stubble guy" and more like, "Wise man who gives advice to young, martial arts prodigy guy."

When my wife Maya sees me with any facial hair, does she complement me on my rugged good looks? No, she says something like, "Honey, why don't you shave? I don't want anyone thinking you're a bum."

Which brings me back to my painful memory.

It is Halloween, 1988. In my desperate desire to act out my "he-man" image, I decide to go to work dressed up like Indiana Jones. I had the leather jacket, the Indy hat, and I even fashioned a rope to look like a leather whip.

Of course, the most important effect was the stubble, and seeing as how this was not an effect I could produce naturally, I opted for some professional makeup to give me the full stubble look. It took 90 minutes to put on but it was worth it.

I walked into the office with everything on, feeling great about myself, when an attractive colleague walked up and said, "Wayne, you look so much better when you let your beard grow out, you really should keep it that way."

Fish, Fish, Where For Art Thou Fish?

I took my son fishing last week, and we almost caught a fish that was THIS big!

Actually, we didn't almost catch anything. Unless, of course, you count seaweed, in which case our fishing expedition was hugely successful.

I've caught my fair share of fish in my day, and I've even caught some big ones, but most of my fishing expeditions have left me empty handed. And while the excitement of pulling in a big catch is certainly real, it's ever so brief and is always sandwiched by hours of staring at a fishing rod, touching worms, and accidentally hooking parts of my body instead of the bait.

So, it came with a little trepidation that I decided to give in to my ten-year old's constant pleading and finally take him out for an afternoon of lake fishing.

Not having fished in years, I decided to make the best of it, and pulled together all the essential tools we would need, which included a lawn chair, picnic umbrella, car magazine, an iPod - and just for good measure I decided to bring along a fishing pole as well.

You could get a sense as to my son's expectations when he went into the garage and pulled out a five gallon bucket to haul away his anticipated bounty of fish. Trying to tamp down expectations, I managed to convince him to bring the toy bucket he used to use in the sandbox when he was two years old.

Once we had arrived at the lake, our next step was to go to the general store next to the lake and pick up some bait, fishing permits, and a five-hour supply of potato chips.

Perhaps my lack of enthusiasm for fishing has less to do with the actual process of fishing as it has to do with the nature of fishing where I live. You see, all the lakes where I live are man-made lakes, which means that the lakes would normally not have any fish in them except for the fact that the city stocks them with fish every season.

Add to the fact that the cost of all the fishing permits and bait on this day cost me over forty dollars, and my afternoon of lake fishing seemed more like going seafood shopping at the local market with an incredibly poor chance of actually bringing home a fish.

Still, trying to be as supportive a Dad as possible, we proceeded down to the lake, where I set up shop – setting up the lawn chair, connecting the picnic umbrella, turning on the iPod, and opening up my first bag of potato chips. Once my "fishing command station" is set up, I realize the fish will not be able to ignore our fishing lines until I first set our rods with hooks and sinkers.

Based on what others were using around the lake, I attach a fake rubber worm to Tyler's pole and mine, and I begin to teach him how to cast his line out into the lake. After having him practice casting a few times without letting the line go, I give him the green light to do it for real. Tyler brought his reel back and tried to fling his line deep into the lake.

After spending 20 minutes untangling the bundle of knots from his first cast, we were ready for attempt number two.

With a few more attempts, my weariness for fishing soon grew into a proud Dad cheering on his son.

"Great cast, Ty! Looking good!"

With a big smile on his face, he reveled in the moment. All of a sudden, his joy of mastering a fishing rod in the water became much more important than whether a fish ever came attached to it.

So while we didn't come home with any big fish, or big fish stories for that matter, at the end of the day we were left with the kind of experience every father and son adventure should have, and I couldn't ask for anything more.

Well that, and I didn't have to clean any fish.

No Crab, But a Barrel Full of Excuses

There's something about fishing, or in my case, crabbing, that brings out the worst in me.

Every year, we head up north to the Pacific Northwest, and every year I go on a fishing or crabbing expedition.

Every year I come up empty handed.

To make things worse, something in my caveman, macho, chromosome Y, DNA makeup requires that prior to any expedition, that I pump up expectations to stratospheric levels.

Maybe I'm exaggerating a bit. Why don't you be the judge.

Here are some of the more interesting boasts, most of which I saved for my wife Maya:

    1) For the crab I'm bringing home tonight, you may need to get a few more gallons of butter.
    2) With the crab I'm bringing back, if a nutcracker doesn't work, maybe we can rent the Jaws of life.
    3) Get set baby – tonight it's not surf and turf! Tonight it's surf and more surf!!!!

Of course, with each roll of my wife's eyes, I become ever more determined to show her that I truly am the king of all things crab.

So, on the final day of our vacation, my friend and I set out to prove that we were more than just talk. We had our crab traps, our bait, our crabbing attire (swimsuit and t-shirt), and a huge plastic bin that was half the size of our inflatable boat.
Yes, I did say "inflatable boat". Upon reflection, it's funny that neither one of us saw the inherent flaw of going out to the open ocean carrying sharp, wire-metal traps looking for spiny legged crabs with sharp pinchers on an inflatable boat. I don't think you'll ever see that on the TV show, "The

Deadliest Catch". But that's another story altogether.

The other thing we didn't consider was checking the Weather Channel before we set out. If we had done that, maybe we would have reconsidered taking a little rubber inflatable boat in the middle of the ocean searching for crab during a torrential rain storm.

As we set our inflatable boat in the water in the pouring rain, the only thought in my head was, "We just have to catch one. Just catch one and I can gloss over everything I said before. All I need is one. Please somebody – just give me one."

If anyone could hear my pleas, it was most likely drowned out by the torrential rain enveloping us, or perhaps they were drowned out by a bevy of crab, mocking us from below.

In either case, we were undeterred. We set our traps, tossed them into the water and waited. And waited. Every time we pulled them up, the traps kept coming up empty, with the only difference being that the traps kept looking cleaner and cleaner each time we pulled them up, as if to emphasize how pristine and "crab-free" the waters were.

After a couple of hours, with the monsoon like rain filling up our dinghy like a cup of tea, we decided to head back…empty handed.

Fortunately, in the 30 minutes it took to row our waterlogged dinghy back to shore, it gave me plenty of time to develop a strategy. It was too late to go to a seafood store and fake it-I'm sure Maya would immediately question why the crab were frozen or why there were rubber bands wrapped around their claws.
I had to think fast. Tell me what you think of my excuses.

1) The torrential rain made me re-think my priorities. I decided to become a Buddhist which means that instead of catching crab, I was practicing mindfulness.

2) There's an old Inuit tradition to eat all the crab on the boat and toss everything overboard when you are done.

3) It was my partner's fault.

4) Once we got into the water, we realized that crabbing season didn't really start until the day after we leave.

5) We actually caught a lot of crab, but in the end, I had a hankering for pizza instead so…

6) I became a vegan. Please re-read excuse #1.

7) We caught plenty of crab, but in good conscience I couldn't permit my friends and family to eat something with such high cholesterol levels, so…

Next year – salmon fishing. Watch out sockeye – here we come!

Dental Work Via Hand Signals

It seems to me that the key to success for any endeavor boils down to one common trait – pride. Parents learn that they should instill a sense of pride in their children for their accomplishments in order to motivate them for the future. An artist's greatest sense of pride comes at the point where they can stand back and bask in the glow of their creation. Pride is what makes each of us aspire to a higher purpose, whether it's going on to college, climbing Mt. Everest, or running for governor after being a professional body builder and the world's highest paid action star.

Yet, pride can come in several forms. Pride for a genuine achievement is a good thing. Pride for pride's sake – not so good. You can see the two faces of pride every week on the TV's American Idol. For every talent like 1st season winner Kelly Clarkson who has earned the right to be proud of her achievement, thousands of other contestants are motivated by their own false sense of pride at their own perceived talents – and often humiliated for their attempt. Unfortunately for the Asian American community, William Hung's recent turn in the limelight is an extreme example of this – let's let it go at that.

Sometimes the difference between genuine and false pride is just a matter of going too far. For example, a genuine sense of pride can be seen from a father who shows off to his kids a birdhouse he built out of an old wooden crate and a broom handle he found in the garage. A false sense of pride comes when the father takes pictures of the same birdhouse and submits them to *Architectural Digest* for review.

I admit that I have been a victim of my own false sense of pride.

Some time ago I needed to find a dentist to fix a few chipped teeth. A good friend recommended his dentist, and I set up an appointment for the following week.

As I checked in, it became apparent to me that everyone in the office – the receptionist, the dentists, even the patients, were all Chinese. Furthermore, as I was led to the dentist's chair, the assistant spoke to me in Chinese, and even handed me some dental literature – again, all in Chinese.

Now, anyone who knows me knows that my Chinese is good enough to exchange pleasantries, order lunch, ask where the bathroom is, or get directions to the nearest airport. Ask me my opinion on say, nuclear proliferation, and my eyes start to glaze over.

As the dentist starts asking me what I need and starts discussing what he will do, any practical person in my position would either a) Tell the dentist that your Chinese isn't that good and ask them to speak English or b) Lunge for the nearest exit as quickly as possible.

However, seeing as how my false sense of pride was in total control (after all, my friend, even though he was from China, used this dentist, therefore, so could I), I proceed to nod repeatedly and respond by saying "Hao" ("Yes" in Chinese) no matter what the dentist asks me. I kept nodding even though what I was hearing sounded like, "First I'm going to yadda yadda yadda, followed by yadda, but yadda yadda hurt much."

In the end, the dentist did manage to fix my chipped teeth by capping them. Unfortunately, I had inadvertently asked that one cap be done in gold, the other in porcelain, and the third in something silver-colored. But hey, I'm still proud of myself.

I'm proud that on clear days, my teeth can tune into some pretty cool radio stations.

Yogurt Schmogurt
- I'll Take Chocolate

In a few days, I will be turning 45 years old. That's over 16,400 days that I have been on this earth. It's funny, because I don't feel a day over 10,000.

I don't feel all that much different than when I was 25 years old. Oh, sure, I've put on a few pounds. My knees ache when I play tennis or go for a run. But for the most part, I still have the same interests, do the same things, and behave pretty much the same way as before.

But the signs of my passing years are all around me. You don't have to look far.

The other day a friend of mine took me to a frozen yogurt shop, which on this Friday night was packed with mostly teens and twenty year olds. It was a self-serve yogurt store, and as I walked in, I immediately noticed the ten machines lined against a wall, each serving two flavors of yogurt, mostly exotic flavors with names like "Taro Tart" and "Asian Peach".

Next to the machines, were containers filled with various toppings, some standards (peanut sprinkles, gummy bears) but many you don't usually associate with toppings (mango slices, sweet red bean, boba).

My friend, who is several years younger than me, started explaining the yogurt phenomenon. "This is a huge craze right now. This latest yogurt boom started in Korea, and now it's all the rage here. There are kids lined up out the door, even around midnight." he said.

The first sign of my advancing years is my disbelief that anyone would stand in line to get frozen yogurt.

"It's just frozen yogurt." I said.

"You've got to try it!" he said.

So, I get in line with everyone else, with nearly 20 people ahead of me, all craning their necks to see when they get to fill their cups with some fruity concoction.

The second sign of my advancing years comes as I fill up my cup and add my toppings. I get to the machine serving "Chocolate" and fill my cup to the top, and then move over to the toppings where I proceed to top my chocolate yogurt with chocolate sprinkles.

As I sit down with my chocolate yogurt with chocolate sprinkles, I take a quick bite, trying to understand what the allure is of what seems to be just an ordinary cup of frozen yogurt.

"I don't get it. It's just frozen yogurt." I say, as I scoop another spoonful into my mouth.

My friend, who suddenly appears completely aghast by my reaction, begins to berate me for my reaction. I don't remember what he said word for word, but it went something like this:

"Well, for heaven's sake, obviously you don't get it! Who comes to a yogurt place that has 20 flavors of yogurt and 200 different toppings and ends up filling their cup with one flavor and one topping of the same flavor?! You're completely clueless! You've got a cup of chocolate yogurt with chocolate sprinkles! Look at my cup! I've got twelve yogurt flavors including mango passionfruit tart, ruby red grapefruit with jalapenos, kiwi pineapple swirl, and Australian papaya infused with blood orange juice and yak meat extract!!!!

"Would it make you feel any better if I added some chocolate syrup to my cup?", I asked.

Of course, when I was growing up, most stores only had three flavors of ice cream – chocolate, vanilla, and strawberry. And yet, somehow, I turned out OK, despite being deprived of Creamy Mochi granola jelly bean yogurt.

So, yes, maybe I'm getting older. But as far as I know, chocolate never really goes out of style.

Blaming Parents For a Happy Childhood

There's an unwritten rule that all parents abide by when raising their children. This rule supercedes all other rules of parenting, whether it is applied intentionally or not. Though the following may not be the formal title of this rule, I believe it is generally recognized as the "When I was a child…" method of parenting.

Comedian Bill Cosby once described how his father invoked this rule when noticing that young Bill was none too eager to walk to school. As I recall, his father said, "When I was a boy, my school was 20 miles away. I walked in bare feet, with 30 pounds of books, uphill…both ways!"

My parents never used the rule intentionally, but then again, they never really had to. Having come from China, my parents both lived in stark conditions devoid of all the conveniences we take for granted today, but there was also the ever constant threat from the Japanese invasion during World War II, as well as the communist takeover of the country. Compared to my childhood in the 70's and 80's in a middle class neighborhood in San Diego, I didn't need many reminders – I knew how fortunate I was – I had a happy childhood.

Of course, this now leads me to my problem. I am now a father, who along with my wife, are raising three kids. While I have every intention to continue the tradition of the "When I was a child…" method as it has been passed down from generation to generation of parents before me, I am having a hard time coming up with appropriate examples of my own that would instill a measure of guilt in my own children. So far, none of the examples I have from my own childhood inspire much sympathy.

I've listed a few examples and you can be the judge. Here goes:

When I was a child, we didn't have a remote control to change the channel on the TV. I had to get up from the sofa to change the channel myself until I started ordering my little brother Steve to be the remote control.

When I was a child, automobiles didn't have child safety restraints or car seats, for that matter. In fact, you weren't even required to wear a seat belt. When we got in the car, my brother and I were usually in the back of our Ford station wagon with the back window rolled all the way down. Any sudden turn would fling us from one side to the other. It was just a part of growing up. Head concussions build character.

When I was a child, public bathrooms didn't have sinks that turned on automatically when you placed your hands in the bowl. Back then, there was a button on top you pressed to get the water started and it only lasted .65 seconds every time you pressed it. In order to wash your hands properly you had to perform an elaborate yoga pose and place one foot on the button to keep the water running.

When I was a child, we didn't get anything fancy for our school lunch. Our menu consisted of bean burritos, fish sticks, soybean hamburgers, and milk. Each day during our lunch break, I would try and open the small, individual sized carton of milk, which was nearly impossible because every time you folded back the carton flap, the spout never opened forcing you to jam a finger into the lip of the container to get any milk. On top of that, the school supplied each of us with one straw made from wax paper, which would immediately go limp after the first sip of milk. Struggling to suck milk through a limp, soggy straw one drop at a time, I'd often black out halfway through the carton.

It's ironic how a happy childhood could lead to a parenting crisis. I'll put some more thought into it after I finish my soybean burger.

The Wild Kingdom - in my Yard

Quiet now. Keep your head down low. Don't take your eyes off him. If he looks your way, keep still.

I know it may sound like I'm currently on a walk-about in some arid Australia outback, but I'm not. I'm not on some African safari either.

But make no mistake about it - I am stalking a wild animal. It's a vile creature intent on tormenting me with it's disgusting, evasive behavior.

I know what you're thinking…if I'm not on a hunting expedition or lost in the woods, what else could I be dealing with? A mountain lion? A bear? Some other kind of varmint?

Specifically, it's a bird that keeps pooping on my new car. I call him the "Turd Raptor" or "Craptor", for short. Now, before you stop reading, let me explain.

I am a reasonable person. When I first noticed that my shiny black car was continually being used literally as a port-a-potty, I reacted in a calm, dispassionate way. After all, I park the car in the driveway of my home, and I park it next to a tree, directly overhead. I was practically asking for it.

It's been going on for weeks. Every morning, as I open up the garage door and walk out to the driveway to my car, I see the latest, in what I would call, "Aviary experimental art", using my car as a canvas.

And to my further dismay, the damage always occurs on the driver's side door. Nowhere else.

As a mature, logical human being, I began to rationally analyze the situation. Obviously, since the damage was always in the same area, and that part of the car was closest to the tree, the offending culprit must have a nest in that area. Knowing that I couldn't fault a mindless bird for doing what it does naturally by building a nest in a tree, I decide that I can easily eliminate the problem of a bird eliminating itself on my car, by moving my car to the other side of the driveway, out from under the tree.

Problem solved, man tames nature. Evolution on display.

Except for the fact that the bird diddled on my car the following morning, and again, did it on the driver's side door, and as if to put a little emphasis on it, added a dollop on the door handle.

The "Craptor" was making this personal.

A few days ago, in an act of desperation, I move my car from the driveway to the street, in a spot that happens to be in front of my house, fully visible from my 2nd floor den. Later that afternoon, as I casually glance from my desk out the window, I finally catch the dirty little flying graffiti artist red handed, er, red winged…well, you know what I mean.

I see an adorable little bird, happily sitting on the luggage rack of my car, pooping on my driver's side window.

Now, every morning I go out to my car, I now bring my briefcase, my keys, a paper towel and a bottle of Windex. The fact that the "sputterages" were always on my driver's side door wherever the car was parked made it obvious that this bird was throwing down the gauntlet. Never one to shrink from a challenge, I start making plans.

Fine by me, you little flying rodent. You want a piece of me? Bring it on. It's man vs. nature. Civilization vs. the wild blue yonder. I'm ready to go "mano a mano". Again, a bird may not have a "mano", but you know what I mean.

I decide to quietly make my way outside to the front yard, and upon seeing the bird sitting on my car, I press the alarm button on my car remote to set the alarm off. The startled bird takes flight, unable to resume it's putrid behavior.

I raise my hands and start doing a victory jig. Man tames nature again. Huzzah, huzzah!

Except, and I am not making this up, the next morning I go out to our other car and see that someone (or more correctly, something) has left their signature mark on that car as well, and I'll give you three guesses where they left it.

Standing next to the car, feeling dejected, and gazing at my tormentor's latest work of art, I realize that I may be beat. I quickly realize that my options are few, it's unlikely that I'll ever be able to catch it, and more importantly, I could never bring myself to harm it in any way.

So what options do I have left? I could only think of one.

If you ever pass by my house, and you see a black SUV with a toy stuffed cat sitting on top of the car, stay quiet and keep your head down low.

I'll be watching.

A Dedication To San Diego's Fire Fighters

I had planned to write the second part of a column I had devoted to a recent trip to Asia, but at this moment, I am on my computer with all my windows closed due to the smoke and ash outside. A few weeks will have passed before you read this but right now, I'm not in a mood to write anything funny, and you may not be in the mood to read it.

I typically write the column with the sole intent of giving those who read it a brief moment to escape from a busy day, usually poking fun at something trivial, often times at my own expense. But to not address the wildfire tragedy would in my mind be like trying to avoid the pink elephant in the room. So much has been lost in such a short period of time.

So, if you would please bear with me, I would like to express some feelings I have of the 2003 wildfires.

We are all at a loss to understand this tragedy. Of the victims, it is impossible to understand the depth of their loss.

Interweaving images: a backdrop of solitary, blackened chimneys, cherished pictures hung on a wall, weary firefighters collapsed by the side of a road, embers alight in a dull sky; are scattered in our thoughts like pieces of a puzzle that put together serve only as a reminder that the firestorm served no higher purpose, or for that matter, any purpose at all.

For many of those who have been spared, the words, "There but for the grace of God…" resounds in their minds. For those who suffered the most, they are left with the task to grieve over loved ones, rebuild their homes and their lives, but also, to rekindle their sense of security. To a greater or lesser degree, as San Diegans and Californians, we all head into the future with trepidation, for we know full well what we have to lose.

There is no security in what is uncertain, as the firestorm certainly was. Perhaps, then, some may find peace in what is constant.

Hour after hour, with the non-stop news coverage, we heard the familiar phrases: *San Diegans are strong. We will rebuild and be better than ever. The community will come together.* The refrains may sound clichéd, but they still ring true.

I believe it comes from a resolve that begins with the firefighters, many of whom were protecting townships and communities they had never before visited, and continues with people who give their time, money, and compassion to benefit families they will never meet.

The *force* of nature has charred property and may have shaken our faith, yet it is from *human* nature where hope resonates. For those who have lost so much, it may at the moment seem like small consolation. But as we rebuild, it is from that resolution where healing begins, where a weary heart may take solace in a community's rising spirit.

Giving a Whole New Meaning to Monkey Business

Evolution of Monkey Picking

I'm sure many of you, like me, were glued to the TV last week, wowed by the spectacle of the opening ceremonies of the 2008 Olympics. The dancers, the special effects, the long procession of athletes walking in to the stadium – I haven't seen a line that long since I stood in line waiting to buy the new iPhone.

Yet, in the days that followed, despite the dominance of swimmer Michael Phelps or the Chinese team's success in gymnastics, the brilliance of the occasion didn't hold my attention as much as a little known company doing business in China that gets very little attention but is actually no less awe-inspiring.

I'm referring, of course, to the tea-picking monkeys of Sichuan.

I learned about the existence of this monkey business during a random meeting a few weeks back. During the meeting, as we were listening to the latest month's sales projections, I glanced over at one of the canisters of tea sitting on the conference table. There, sitting next to the other nondescript teas, was a canister of tea called, "The Monkey Picked Ti Kuan Yin".

In the description, it read:

The legend of tea-plucking monkeys comes from the inaccessibility of mountain grown teas. Nurtured by clouds and mist, Ti Kuan Yin has an intense aroma and a complex, long-lasting finish.

In that moment, all my thoughts about the meeting disappeared and at once I became intrigued at the idea that in my tea cup, I was drinking tea made from tea leaves plucked by a monkey in a forest thousands of miles away.

A few thoughts: 1) How did the tea farmer initially decide that they were going to use animals to help them pluck tea leaves and how did they end up with a monkey? I mean, at some point someone came to the conclusion, "OK, no more ladders. No more long poles with knives on the end. From here on in, we're using animals. Now where can we find a monkey?"

Actually, my guess is that they had to work their way up to a monkey. I mean, why go through the cost and effort of acquiring a monkey when, say, a squirrel can climb a tree just as well as a monkey and is already climbing your tea trees?

In an attempt to confirm my hypothesis, I'm planning to employ the local squirrels in my backyard for a little manual labor. While I have no tealeaf plants for them to pick, I figure that they are perfectly suited to clean out the gutters of my house. I will report on my progress with this at a later date.

Now back to the monkeys.

At some point, the tea farmer decides to use monkeys to pick tea leaves. So, my next question is, how do you train a monkey to pluck tea leaves?

Now don't get me wrong, I know that monkeys are capable of doing a lot of things – carnival tricks, sign language, etc., but picking tea leaves?

I imagine the training sessions involve a lot of frustration and patience for the tea farmer.

Bungo! Get over here! Drop that banana and get over here now! How many times do I have to tell you? I only want tea leaves! Nothing else! What did you bring me this time? A shoe! One shoe! You've been monkeying around all day! Today alone you've brought me three tea leaves, a rock, four sticks, a dead mouse and this shoe. Bungo! Stop scratching yourself and pay attention! You never see Bingo, Bango or Devin making these kind of mistakes. Now you shape up or no more bananas and you can go back into the jungle to eat bananas whenever you want! Get back to work you cotton-pickin', tea-leaf pickin' monkey!

The funny thing is that this company is actively promoting their tea and how monkeys picked the tea leaves. I wonder how it would go over here if the next time you pick a bottle of ketchup and in bold print it read, "The finest ketchup made from tomatoes picked by our own band of monkeys!"

Last thought: now that the Chinese have proven themselves in gymnastics while still having monkeys climbing tea leaves from trees humans can't climb, wouldn't this be the perfect time for the ultimate face off?

Now that's a sporting event I'd pay to go see.

Kope Coffee Truly Scat-terbrained Idea

Sometimes these columns just kind of write themselves.

A few weeks ago I wrote about some tealeaf plucking monkeys in China that supposedly know how to pick tealeaves when they are good and ready. With my active mind, I immediately conjured up thoughts of the training process involved in training monkeys to pluck and deliver tea leaves and not other things like, say, a pair of shoes hanging from a telephone wire, an errant hub cap, or an old TV guide from the 1970's.

But that bit of primate/beverage trivia can't hold a candle to the latest beverage I've recently discovered.

A few days ago, a friend of mine dropped by and our conversation went something like this:

Friend: Sorry I'm a little late but I had a hard time getting up. I feel sick.

Me: What's the matter?

Friend: Well, last night my wife made some coffee we got from a friend who just came back from a trip to Asia. I had some last night and I've had a headache ever since.

Me: Does it have a lot of caffeine? What kind of coffee is it?

Friend: It's called Kopi Luwak, and it comes from Indonesia. It's really expensive, almost $300/pound.

Me: I think I'd get a headache just paying for $300.00 coffee.

Friend: No, it's supposed to be special. There are these squirrel-like animals call Luwaks who eat the coffee beans and something happens to the bean while it's in it's stomach, and once the Luwaks leave their droppings, the harvesters pick them up, clean it off and...

Me: Whoa! Whoa! Whoa! Backup, backup, backup...

OK. You are now up to speed.

The rest of the conversation consisted of my friend telling me that the stomach acid in the Luwak's intestines supposedly enhances the flavor of the bean so that the coffee is extra smooth with a slightly bitter aftertaste.

This, of course, was not where my attention was focused.

I am, by no means, a prude. I have consumed turtles, rattlesnakes, pigeons, alligators, and even tea plucked by the afore mentioned Chinese monkeys. But even being the reasonably adventurous person I am, I still have major reservations out of drinking coffee brewed from the beans extruded (excreted?) from the bowels of an Indonesian squirrel!

I've always been fascinated with the origins of various activities, and this one especially.

At some point, someone was walking around Indonesia, perhaps a farmer, or maybe even someone who was cleaning up their backyard. The person sees the Luwak scat all over the yard, and suddenly has an epiphany.

"Wait a minute! We could pick up this scat, clean off the beans and make coffee with it! Nothing like killing two birds with one, er, bean!" Apparently, they didn't consider other potential uses of it (fertilizer, a game of jacks, paperweights, scat-fights, etc.) – no, they decided to clean off the beans and drink it.

Which brings up an important question: how clean is clean enough? If I were shopping for some Kopi Luwak coffee, I'd have some serious sanitation queries.

Yes, could you tell me about this bag of Kopi Luwak coffee? How is it washed? Water? That's it? No bleach? No sulfuric acid? No radioactive wave treatments? Hmm...I think I'll pass.

On the other hand, the existence of this coffee shouldn't really surprise anyone. We live in an age where capitalism is king, and we have become a population interested in all things new. If it's something new, people want it and they will pay through the nose to get it.

Wait a minute! We have pets. I could be sitting on a goldmine.

CPSIA information can be obtained at www.ICGtesting.com
Printed in the USA
BVOW060245130612

292522BV00003B/144/P